English for the Teacher

CAMBRIDGE TEACHER TRAINING AND DEVELOPMENT

Series Editors: Marion Williams and Tony Wright

This series is designed for all those involved in language teacher training and development: teachers in training, trainers, directors of studies, advisers, teachers of in-service courses and seminars. Its aim is to provide a comprehensive, organised and authoritative resource for language teacher training and development.

Teach English – A training course for teachers
by Adrian Doff

Models and Metaphors in Language Teacher Training –
Loop input and other strategies*
by Tessa Woodward

Training Foreign Language Teachers – A reflective approach
by Michael J. Wallace

Literature and Language Teaching – A guide for teachers and trainers*
by Gillian Lazar

Classroom Observation Tasks – A resource book for language
teachers and trainers*
by Ruth Wajnryb

Tasks for Language Teachers – A resource book for training*
and development
by Martin Parrott

English for the Teacher – A language development course*
by Mary Spratt

Teaching Children English – A training course for teachers of English*
to children
by David Vale with Anne Feunteun

A Course in Language Teaching – Practice and theory
by Penny Ur

Looking at Language Classrooms
A teacher development video package

About Language – Tasks for teachers of English
by Scott Thornbury

Action Research for Language Teachers
by Michael J. Wallace

Mentor Courses – A resource book for trainer-trainers
by Angi Malderez and Caroline Bodóczky

* Original Series Editors: Ruth Gairns and Marion Williams

English for the Teacher

A language development course

Mary Spratt

CAMBRIDGE
UNIVERSITY PRESS

PUBLISHED BY THE PRESS SYNDICATE OF THE UNIVERSITY OF CAMBRIDGE
The Pitt Building, Trumpington Street, Cambridge, United Kingdom

CAMBRIDGE UNIVERSITY PRESS
The Edinburgh Building, Cambridge CB2 2RU, UK
40 West 20th Street, New York, NY 10011–4211, USA
477 Williamstown Road, Port Melbourne, VIC 3207, Australia
Ruiz de Alarcón 13, 28014 Madrid, Spain
Dock House, The Waterfront, Cape Town 8001, South Africa

http://www.cambridge.org

First published 1994
Eighth printing 2002

Printed in the United Kingdom at the University Press, Cambridge

A catalogue record for this book is available from the British Library

Library of Congress Cataloguing in Publication data
Spratt, Mary.
    English for the teacher: a language development course/Mary Spratt
        p. cm.   (Cambridge teacher training and development)
    ISBN 0 521 42676 6 (pbk.)
    1. English language – Study and teaching – Foreign speakers.
    2. English language   Textbooks for foreign speakers.
    3. English teachers   Training of.
    4. Teachers, Foreign.
    I. Title.
    II. Series
    PE1128.A2S67   1994   93-34970
    428′.007 – dc 20   CIP

ISBN 0 521 42676 6 Book
ISBN 0 521 42677 4 Cassette

Contents

Thanks

The author would like to thank Ruth Gairns and Brigit Viney for all their support and advice on the project. Thanks too to Sue Ellis and to those who undertook the reading and piloting of the project. Finally, many thanks to Margaret Callow of the Bell College, Saffron Walden and those Bell College students who contributed so helpfully to the 'Student Language' section of this book.

Acknowledgements

The authors and publishers are grateful to the authors, publishers and others who have given their permission for the use of copyright material identified in the text. While every endeavour has been made, it has not been possible to identify the sources of all material used and in such cases the publishers would welcome information from copyright owners.

Photographs and illustrations
Adrian Warren/Ardea London Ltd. for pic.1 on p.7; Ardea London Ltd. for pic.2 on p.7; P. Morris/Ardea London Ltd. for pic.3 on p.7; Guzelian Photography for pics. 1 and 2 on p.22; Tony Morrison/South American Pictures for pic.3 on p.22; Kreuger/Zefa for pic.4 on p.22; Newcastle Chronicle and Journal Ltd. for pic.1 on p.37; Guzelian Photography for pic.2 on p.37; Zefa for pics. 3 and 4 on p.37; Guzelian Photography for pic.1 on p.63; John Gittings for pic. 2 on p.63; Zefa for pic.3 on p.63; Jeremy Pembrey for all pics. on p.69; Al Francekevich/Zefa for p.88; Mary Evans Picture Library for pics.1 and 2 on p.95; Guzelian Photography for pic.3 on p.95; David Cummings/Eye Ubiquitous for pic.4 on p.95; Milton Road Infants' School, Cambridge for p.102; David Cummings/Eye Ubiquitous for p.110; Nigel Luckhurst for all pics. on p.115; Zefa for p.120.

Text extracts
Times Educational Supplement for the article on p.8 'Young gain most from exchanges' © Times Newspapers Ltd. 22.3.91; Macmillan Publishers Ltd. for the adapted extract on p.19 from *C.L.L. (Community Language Learning) – A Way Forward?* by Rod Bolitho in ELT Documents 113; George Weidenfeld & Nicolson Ltd. for the adapted extracts on pp. 22–4 and 127–8 from *Teachers* by Frank E. Hugget; Longman Group Ltd. for the questionnaire on pp.31–2 from *Making the Most of Your Textbook* by Neville Grant; Newspaper Publishing for the article on p.38 'Teaching with a magic touch' © The Independent on Sunday 23.3.90; The British Council for the articles on p.42 'About England', 'Role plays' and 'Describing people – games and activities' which appeared in *The British Council Newsletter for Portuguese Teachers of English* March 1986 and Spring 1990 and for the extract from the article on p.49 'People are like that' which appeared in *Fun Press* December 1990; Mary Glasgow Publications Ltd. for the adapted article on pp.54–5 'Teacher development explained' which appeared in *Practical English Teaching* June 1990 © Mary Glasgow Publications Ltd., London; IATEFL for the conference programme on p.59; The University of Edinburgh for the extracts on pp.64–5 from *The Best Years* edited by J.M. Hughes; *Options* for the quotations on p.69; The National Exhibition of Children's Art for the poems on p.74 'Memories of a vegetable' and 'An old woman' from *Cadbury's Fifth Book of Poetry*; Pieta Monks for the article on p.81 'A tale of two teachers' which appeared in *The Teacher* (the official journal of the National Union of Teachers) Jan./Feb. 1993; British Srl, Genoa, Italy for the advertisement on p.83 'EFL teachers'; Walker & Walker for the advertisement on p.83 'Emigrate/Work abroad'; David English House for the advertisement on p.83 'Japan'; VSO and L.C.R. Advertising for the advertisement on p.83 'Time for a change and a new challenge?'; Buckswood International School for the advertisement on p.85; Maggie Drummond for the article on p.89 'A day in the life of a teacher' which appeared in *Options* October 1990; Serpent's Tail, 4 Blackstock Mews, London, N4 2BT for the extract on pp.96–7 from *Forties Child* by Tom Wakefield © Tom Wakefield 1980; Central Bureau for Educational Visits and Exchanges for the advertisement on p.100; Routledge & Kegan Paul for the extract on p.103 from *Troublesome Children* by Irene Caspari; Sunday Times Magazine for the extract on pp.104–5 from 'Just another day at Jefferson High' by Russell Miller © Times Newspapers Ltd. 29.3.92; Sue Surkes for the extract on p.106 from 'Sarcasm – the lowest form of discipline' which appeared in the *Times Educational Supplement* 17.3.89; Mary Glasgow Publications Ltd. for the extract on p.107 from 'Classroom discipline' which appeared in *Practical English Teaching* December 1989 © Mary Glasgow Publications Ltd., London; Barbara Monda for the article on p.108 'What makes a good English teacher?' which appeared in *Fun Press* December 1992; Newsweek for the article on p.114 by Barbara Kantrowitz and Pat Wingert and for the illustration on p.114 © 24.2.92 Newsweek Inc. All rights reserved. Reprinted by permission; Express Newspapers plc for the article on p.120 'Playaholic's frantic fun courts death' the *Sunday Express* 23.6.91; A.M. Heath for the adapted extract on p.124 from *Apes, Men and Language* by Eugene Linden; Radio Telefís Éireann for the extracts and recordings on p.126; Peter Maingay for the extract and recording on p.129 © Peter Maingay; Martin Brown for the adapted article on pp.131–2 'Nothing wrong in the state of Denmark' which appeared in *The Teacher* Spring 1990.

Drawings by David Downton and George Taylor.

Map of the book

Vocabulary area	Grammar
Components of communication	
Teaching and learning activities	The past simple, past perfect and past continuous tenses
Description of a teaching situation	*Used to* and *would* for past habits
Coursebook description and evaluation	The past simple tense contrasted with the present perfect tense
Classroom activities	The perfect tenses
Relationships and feelings	Relative clauses
Teacher development and teacher training	Indirect commands
Teacher and learner behaviour	The second conditional
Adjectives of attitude Teaching activities	Personal plans, intentions, predictions and certainties
Terms and conditions of work	Comparatives and superlatives of adjectives
Teaching duties and activities	Questions
Character description	The third conditional
Classroom discipline and classroom management	The definite article
Character adjectives Classroom behaviour	Tag questions and indirect questions
Free time activities Stress	Some modal verbs

Map of the book

		Functions	Classroom instructions
Part 1: Introductions	1	Agreeing and disagreeing	Introducing a listening activity
	2	Expressions of hesitation, self-correcting, rephrasing, stopping interruptions	Introducing a conversation lesson
	3	Showing interest, sympathy and admiration	Introducing a reading activity
Part 2: Inside the English language classroom	4	Changing the subject	Introducing a writing activity
	5	Introducing ideas, agreeing, clarifying, concluding	Preparing for a speaking activity
	6	Inviting opinions	Giving instructions for homework
Part 3: Development	7	Making suggestions and expressing preferences	Introducing a true/false listening activity
	8	Asking for clarification	Introducing a grammar activity
	9	Expressing plans, predictions and certainties	Introducing a role play
Part 4: Being a teacher	10	Expressing uncertainty and enthusiasm	Introducing pronunciation work
	11	Asking questions	Introducing pair work
	12	Asking questions	Introducing a vocabulary activity
Part 5: Wider educational issues	13	Introducing opinions	Introducing pair correction
	14	Checking agreement	Introducing a gap-filling activity
	15	Linking ideas in a conversation	Introducing a discussion activity

Student language	Reflections on teaching
Assessing oral communication	Useful/enjoyable activities
Assessing written work	Teaching/learning techniques
Assessing oral communication	The value of talking about yourself in class
Assessing written work	The ideal coursebook
Assessing written work	Classroom activities
Assessing oral communication	Relationships at school
Assessing written work	Teacher development
Assessing written work	Encouraging student development
Assessing oral communication	Using role play
Assessing written work	Job satisfaction
Assessing oral communication	Activities needing organisation
Assessing oral communication	Activities suitable for your students
Assessing written work	Evaluating lessons
Assessing oral communication	Discrimination in the classroom
Assessing oral communication	Teaching through topics

Introduction

1   Who is this book for?

English for the Teacher is a language improvement course for teachers of English as a Foreign Language whose first language is not English. It focusses particularly on the language that teachers need for use in the classroom, for talking and reading about their work and for furthering their studies in English as a Foreign Language. It can be used by in-service or pre-service teachers, by teachers attending courses or by teachers studying on their own.

2   What is the level of this book?

Generally speaking, this book is intended for teachers whose language is at good intermediate or a more advanced level. However, as teachers often have more varied language-learning histories than many students of general English, this book has a more open approach to level than many coursebooks used by these students.

3   What are the aims of this book?

The primary aim of this book is to provide teachers with a means for developing and extending their use of English with particular emphasis on English related to teaching. It focusses on the English needed in the following areas:

- in the classroom
- for studying the teaching and learning of English as a Foreign Language
- for participating in teacher development and teacher-training courses
- for making work-related contacts
- for taking part in work-related discussions.

For example, it contains reading and listening texts related to topics such as language learning, talking about lessons, organising your time, student development and gender in the classroom. It also contains sections that focus on the language of classroom instructions, and others that look at how to assess students' oral and written language.

The book also aims to:

- provide teachers with opportunities to read about, listen to, reflect on and discuss issues related to teaching and learning
- allow teachers to be learners and have the opportunity, through reflection on the learning methods they use, to better understand their own teaching and learning styles
- allow teachers to evaluate the benefit for their own students of different learning activities and approaches to learning
- allow teachers to feel more confident in their use of English.

4 What is in this book?

Parts

English for the Teacher contains fifteen units which are organised into five parts, according to the following broad themes:

- Introductions
- Inside the English language classroom
- Development
- Being a teacher
- Wider issues.

These themes have been chosen as being central to most teachers' work and as representing subjects which teachers are frequently involved in discussing, reading, thinking about or following up in other ways. Through these themes the book aims to bring in and explore language of particular relevance to language teachers.

Units and sections

The units are topic-based and focus on subjects such as: teacher development, coursebooks, a teacher's character. Each unit is self-contained, and includes the following sections in varying order:

- Starter activities
- Listening
- Reading
- Speaking
- Writing
- Grammar
- Student language
- Classroom instructions
- Conclusions.

These sections have been included in the book on a systematic basis in order to provide regular and integrated coverage of the four language skills, opportunities for the study of the language system, and ways of developing teaching-related language, as well as awareness and evaluation of teaching methodologies. Each section develops out of the previous one, and consists of an integrated sequence of activities. The aim and content of each section is described below.

STARTER ACTIVITIES

This section, which occurs at the beginning of each unit, is designed to stimulate discussion of the new topic and relate it personally to the reader.

SPEAKING, READING, WRITING, LISTENING

The main focus of each of these sections is obviously the relevant language skill. Each skill is, however, treated in an integrated way and contains activities that bring in other language skills and a focus on language subskills.

GRAMMAR

The structures chosen as the focus for each of the grammar sections have been selected as representing areas that are central to language use and that can also be problem areas. The approach is generally an exploratory one that asks readers to rely on and activate their prior knowledge. This approach has been adopted in preference to one which is more explicit in presenting information about grammar. This is because, unlike many EFL students, the readers of this book will normally have studied these grammatical points before and probably do not need to be presented with information about them. Opportunities to reflect on and work out rules of grammar, as well as apply them, can be more valuable for these readers.

STUDENT LANGUAGE

The activities used in these sections of the book vary considerably in that sometimes they concentrate on grammar, sometimes on pronunciation, sometimes on overall impression, etc. The purpose of this section is to provide readers with an opportunity to examine their attitudes to student error, the value and role of error and also how and when to correct students. While doing this, they will also often have opportunities to work on language accuracy.

CLASSROOM INSTRUCTIONS

Classroom instructions form a major part of teacher talking time in a classroom, yet often the language of these instructions is not taught. Teachers have to pick it up or work it out as best they can. This section provides an opportunity for a systematic focus on classroom language. Each section provides a set of instructions that could be used to introduce one of the activities in the unit. The activities that have been chosen represent ones that are very common in the classroom, e.g. introducing a reading activity, giving instructions for homework, introducing pair work. The instructions are presented as a cloze test; the words that have been removed are usually prepositions, particles, articles, demonstrative pronouns or key lexical items. In this way readers are given the opportunity to concentrate on the linguistic accuracy of instructions. Readers are then asked to give the same instructions in their own words, if preferred, so that they can extend the accuracy practice to their own use of language.

CONCLUSIONS

This section always contains two activities: *Teaching-related vocabulary* and *Reflections on teaching* (see below).

Activities

A wide variety of activities is used to focus on the four language skills. These include classifying, prioritising, true/false, selecting, listing, giving definitions, matching, note-taking, role-play, consensus discussion, opinion-gap activities, letter and article writing and many others. These activities have been chosen to provide variety and to allow the skill to be focussed on in the most authentic or appropriate way, e.g. work on subskills such as pronunciation, reading for specific information, listening for gist, etc.

Examples of regularly occurring activities are:

TALKING POINTS

This activity occurs regularly as the final part of the exploitation of a reading or listening text. It is presented simply as a list of discussion points which can be talked about in groups or pairs or in whole-class discussion. There is no need to discuss all of the points. In other words, the *Talking points* are intended to be used flexibly.

LANGUAGE FUNCTIONS

In most units there is an activity which focusses on particular language functions, e.g. advising, giving and asking for clarification, changing the subject. This activity is designed to provide teachers with the chance to meet, study and use language which is often colloquial and very common in spoken language, yet not often presented in grammar books. It is an important ingredient of classroom language and its appropriate and fluent use contributes considerably to the naturalness of language.

TEACHING-RELATED VOCABULARY

This activity occurs in the *Conclusions* section at the end of each unit. Its aim is to allow for recall and extension of the topic-related vocabulary that has occurred in the unit.

REFLECTIONS ON TEACHING

This activity also occurs at the end of each unit. It poses questions about the topic or learning activities of the unit. It gives readers an opportunity for reflection on the value of the topic or activities to themselves and to their own students; in other words it provides moments to reflect on the content of the unit and on the extent of its learning value.

Authentic texts

The *Reading, Listening* and *Student language* sections are structured round authentic texts. The written student texts are all taken from students' homework, classwork, or articles or stories submitted to school magazines. The students' oral language comes from recordings of students carrying out classroom activities. Other texts also cover a large range of text types. For example, the reading texts include articles from magazines and newspapers, extracts from novels and autobiographies, advertisements, poems, letters and conference programmes. The listening texts include conversations, talks and interviews with people of varying ages, nationalities and backgrounds.

The texts developed in the productive skills sections of speaking and writing also have an authentic focus. Readers are asked to write letters of various kinds, articles, book reviews, etc. and to engage in discussions and conversations.

Reference material

By way of reference material the book includes:

- Tapescripts of all the materials on the cassette, i.e. the listening texts and oral student language for assessment.
- An Answer Key which provides the answers to all the objective tasks in the book. It does not give answers to questions which depend on judgement or experience.

5 How to use this book

The units

The Map of the Book on pages viii–xi shows the detailed content of each unit. Use this to decide what to do next. Although the units are grouped thematically each one works independently, so you can use the book in a variety of ways. e.g.:

- Work through the book from beginning to end.
- Select units in accordance with your particular needs and interests
- Concentrate on particular sections across units, e.g. *Student language, Classroom instructions, Grammar.*

Notes for teachers using the book alone

Teachers working alone will be able to carry out the great majority of the activities in the book, and use the Answer Key to get feedback on their progress on objective tasks. The instructions to some activities ask readers to work in pairs or groups, or to compare and discuss answers. These are useful classroom activities, but they do not prevent the reader working alone from using them in part at least. Choose those parts of each activity which you feel you can carry out by yourself. Even speaking activities can be done alone. Talking aloud to yourself can do much to develop your confidence, fluency, pronunciation and accuracy.

Notes for trainers

How you use this book and what you choose to use in it will depend very much on the interests and needs of the group of teachers you are working with. The book has been designed so it can be used flexibly on a dip-in basis at unit level. The sections and activities are more closely linked and, with the exception of the *Starter activities*, *Student language*, *Classroom instructions* and *Grammar* sections, lend themselves more to sequential treatment.

This book is about both language improvement and issues related to teaching. One or both of these strands can be emphasised in a lesson or across a series of lessons. In its informal approach to issues related to teaching, the book can provide a useful tool in teacher development and an introduction to and general familiarisation with methodology.

In order to involve participants on your courses further in this book and in their exploration of language and methodology, you may find it useful to ask them to bring in supplementary materials, e.g. magazine articles, examples of their own students' language, transcripts and recordings of their own classroom instructions.

English for the Teacher has been piloted in various parts of the world with a range of different teachers. The author would like to thank them and all those teachers with whom she has worked during her career for the many enjoyable and thought-provoking hours she has shared with them.

Cambridge, UK
June 1993

Symbols

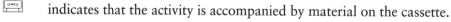

indicates that the activity is accompanied by material on the cassette.

O⚷ indicates that answers to the activity are provided in the Answer Key.

1   About communication

1   Starter activities

1 Look at the pictures. Do you think these animals are communicating? What might they be saying?

2 Look at the list below and tick those things which humans use to communicate with each other. Then compare your answers with a partner.

style of dress   body posture
gestures   fluency
listening   hair style
facial expressions   vocabulary
accurate use of language structures   behaviour
eye movements   accent

3 In your opinion, which of the items in the list above contribute most to communication? Number the five most important (1 = most important). Then compare your answers with a partner.

2   Reading

1 If your students of English went on an exchange trip to an English-speaking country for a month, which aspect of their communication in English would you expect to improve most? Choose from the list below and then discuss your choices with a partner.

accent   accuracy in use of language structures
vocabulary   other (please specify)
fluency

2 Now read the article below which reports research findings on the language benefits of exchange trips for teenagers. Does it confirm your opinions?

Young gain most from exchanges

Younger pupils benefit most from exchange language trips to France, a research project has concluded. It confirms that all pupils' performances in French improve as the result of an exchange trip, *writes Diane Spencer.*

Dr Kate Seager from the School Examinations and Assessment Council carried out a three-year study of just over 100 pupils to test their French language skills following cross-Channel visits.

Five groups were aged 17 to 19 and five were in the 13 and 14 age band. Visits lasted between nine days and a month.

Dr Seager was able to report on accent, accuracy, fluency, vocabulary and language structures. She found that the average overall improvement in language performance of most of the pupils tested after one month's stay was between 20 and 25 per cent and after the shorter stay it was 13.5 per cent.

However, a longer stay did not always result in a higher improvement in all linguistic aspects tested. The fluency of 17- to 19-year-olds who had stayed nine days had improved by about 19 per cent whereas for those staying a month the improvement was about 15 per cent.

Younger pupils showed a greater improvement in accuracy, between 21.5 and 25 per cent, than older ones who improved by 13.6 per cent after nine days and 19 per cent after a month.

She noted 'dramatic improvements' in both age groups in the use of vocabulary and adjectives: about 38 per cent for both age groups for adjectives and in vocabulary, 17 per cent for the older students for the short stay and 49 per cent for the young ones after a month.

But there was less success with accent: only a 4.5 per cent average improvement. More than two-thirds retained the same score after the visit, 'indicating that the accent acquired when first learning the language is, for the most part, retained'.

'At a time of an acute shortage of modern language teachers, it is important not to compromise on the accent of any teacher, but above all the teacher who introduces the language,' commented Dr Seager.

(from The Times Educational Supplement)

3 Look at the words below. Put a dot (•) above the stressed syllable in each word or group of words.

a) exchange trip   e) fluency   i) improvement
b) performance   f) vocabulary   j) adjectives
c) accent   g) structures
d) accuracy   h) average

Now check your answers with the cassette and repeat the words.

Explain the meaning of (a) – (j) to a partner as if you were talking to a group of intermediate students. For example:

A: What does X mean?
B: Well, . . .

4 Read the article again and complete the chart below which summarises the research.

Number of pupils tested	*Just over 100*
Number of groups in study	
Age range of groups	
Amount of overall language improvement after stay of: • one month • less than one month	
Improvements in: • fluency • accuracy • vocabulary • accent	*15–19%*

5 Talking points

Talk about one or two of the points below with a partner or partners.

• Do any of these research findings surprise you?

• Why do you think accent seems to improve less than other aspects of communication?

• What benefits might you yourself get out of an exchange trip?

• Discuss the benefits of any exchange trips you have heard about.

3   Writing: A letter

1 Read the advertisements below for student exchange trips. Which would be best for your students? Why? Discuss the reasons for your choice with a partner.

> My students and I would very much like to set up a penfriend scheme with students from Scotland and then arrange an exchange or visit programme. They are aged 13–14, and we live in a beautiful, sunny and historical town in Portugal. The people here are also very friendly.
> **Pedro Alvarez, Rua de Misericordia 55, Evora, Portugal**
>
> I work with adult students of English. We are very interested in making contact with other adult learners to make friends, exchange ideas and information and also arrange exchange visits.
> **Carmen Perez, Calle Oriental 102, Punta Arenas, Chile**
>
> I'm a teacher of English to primary-school students aged between 7 and 11. I'd like to make contact with a UK primary teacher so that our students could exchange letters and visits.
> **Ursula Seitl, Bajcsy – Zs u 29, Budapest, Hungary**

2 Now write a letter replying to the advertisement that interests you most, or write your own advertisement.

4   Student language: Assessing oral communication

1 You are going to listen to a conversation between two students: a Japanese woman and a Spanish man. Listen and find out the subject of their conversation and their general level of English.

2 Listen again and complete the chart opposite. Give each student a score for their ability in each aspect of communication (0 = poor, 1 = fair, 2 = good, 3 = excellent). Then discuss your assessments with a partner.

	Japanese woman	*Spanish man*	*You*
Pronunciation (sounds, stress, intonation)			
Vocabulary			
Accurate use of language structures			
Fluency			

3 If you were these students' teacher, what aspect of communication would you try and help them with most? Why? Discuss.

4 Complete the last column of the chart with an assessment of your own ability to communicate in English. Which of the aspects of communication listed here would you most like to improve? Discuss your language needs with a partner.

5   Listening

1 You are going to listen to an excerpt from a documentary programme about two characters called Booee and Bruno. Listen and find out why the title of the programme is *Communication with a Difference*.

2 Listen again and complete the summary of the excerpt below.

> Booee and Bruno are two (*a*) ………. . They 'speak' using a language called (*b*) ………. which is a (*c*) ………. language. It contains (*d*) ………. cheremes and has a (*e*) ………. of its own.
>
> The chimpanzees have been taught Ameslan as part of an (*f*) ………. to see if language is (*g*) ………. to humans. Another chimpanzee, Ally, has been taught (*h*) ………. as well as Ameslan.
>
> Because of the linguistic successes of the chimpanzees some scientists are now wondering whether the reason why chimpanzees don't speak is (*i*) ………. rather than neurological.

3 Do you think that chimpanzees can communicate in the same way as humans, or is language unique to humans? Discuss with a partner.

6 Speaking

1 Read the statements below about communication. Put a tick next to those you agree with and a cross next to those you disagree with.

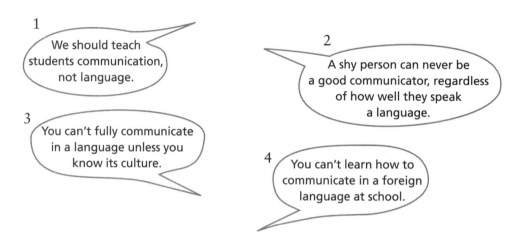

1 We should teach students communication, not language.

2 A shy person can never be a good communicator, regardless of how well they speak a language.

3 You can't fully communicate in a language unless you know its culture.

4 You can't learn how to communicate in a foreign language at school.

2 Language functions

Read the expressions below and then put them into two groups: *expressions of agreement* and *expressions of disagreement*.

I doubt it.	That's just not the case.
Right.	I don't agree.
That's very unlikely.	Exactly.
Absolutely.	That's it.

Add any other expressions you know, and then compare your lists with a partner's.

3 Discuss your answers to Activity 1 above with a partner, using as many of the expressions of agreement and disagreement that you find appropriate.

7 Classroom instructions: Introducing a listening activity

1 A teacher might introduce Section 5, Activity 2, on page 11 with the following instructions. Read them and then fill in the blanks.

'OK, now this time we're going to listen (*a*) .... the excerpt again but in greater detail. I want (*b*) .... to (*c*) .... the summary of the excerpt as you listen. OK? That's right, fill (*d*) .... the blanks in this passage.

'Now, before you listen again, (*e*) .... you read the summary to make (*f*) .... you understand it and to know what you're listening (*g*) .... ? If there are any words you don't understand, just (*h*) .... me.'

2 Now introduce the same activity to a partner as if you were speaking to a class. Use your own words or those above.

8 Conclusions

1 Teaching-related vocabulary

Look at the chart below which lists some of the kinds of activities in this unit. Find the activities in the unit and complete the first column of the chart with the correct section and activity number. Compare your answers with a partner.

	Section and activity number	Most enjoyable	Most useful
Reading for detail	2.2, 2.4		
Work on word stress			
Fluency practice			
Self-awareness activities			
A gap-filling activity			
An opinion-gap activity			
Letter writing			

2 Reflections on teaching

- Complete the remaining columns in the chart above. Number the activities from 1 to 7 (1 = most enjoyable/useful, 7 = least enjoyable/ useful). Then discuss your answers with a partner.

- What can you conclude from your answers for yourself as a learner? And for your teaching?

2 About language learning

1 Starter activities

1 Look at the statements from students below. They are about the ways in which they like or dislike learning languages. Put a tick next to those you agree with and a cross next to those you disagree with.

1

2

I don't like just hearing the language – I really need to see it written too.

3

I just like to hear the foreign language for a long time before I speak.

4

I like to go to the foreign country and talk, talk, talk – mistakes and all.

5

I like to talk first with other students who are trying to learn like me.

6

I don't like learning grammar – it's boring and it confuses me.

I hate it when people correct my mistakes.

2 Draw two more bubbles and write in them two other statements about the way in which you like or dislike learning languages. Then compare your answers with a partner.

2 Listening

1 Listen to Emmah, right, talking about how she learnt French at school in Britain and how she would like to learn French in future. Decide which of the statements above she would agree with.

2 Listen again and make notes in the chart below. Then compare your answers with a partner.

The ways in which Emmah learnt French at school	The ways in which Emmah would like to learn French	
	At school	*In France*
Written work		

3 Look at the list below of words and expressions from the conversation. With a group, write definitions of each one. Then explain them to someone from a different group, as if you were explaining them to a student. Would you explain them just by using the definition or in some other way?

verb tables   slang
to learn off by heart   picking up a language

3 Speaking

1 Language functions

Look at the expressions below. They are all expressions you can use to keep going while you are talking. Put them into three groups: *expressions of hesitation, expressions for correcting yourself/rephrasing,* and *expressions to stop interruptions.*

now, let me think	what I mean is
I mean	I just wanted to add
hold on	how can I put it?
sorry, what I meant to say was . . .	or rather
just a minute	

2 Now discuss with a partner:

- how you learnt English
- if the way you learnt was a good way
- if the way you teach is influenced by the way you learnt English.

Try to use the expressions above at appropriate places in your discussion.

4   Student language: Assessing written work

1 The short composition below was written by a student. Read it through quickly. What is it about?

I'd had a lot of teachers that I liked so much, but it was a long time ago and I can't remember really. But recently I'd had a teacher and I think I'll never forget her. She wasn't extraordinary. She was a normal person.

She was confident about her. She didn't want to show us good/bad things/feelings about her. She wanted only to teacher. She decided 'You have to learn this' and she was going straight on! She had a good way to teach and could understand our weaknesses. She always was trying to find the best way. Before or after grammar's lessons she tried to show us how and why learn this lesson, with some practical joke (examples).

Everyone was enjoying her lessons. No one wanted the end of the class.

But I think she was so good because before teaching something for someone she thought 'If I didn't know this, how I would like that someone teach to me? Which is the best way?'

2 Correct the mistakes underlined in the composition.

3 In mistakes (a), (c), (e), (f) and (g) the student has used the wrong tense. Why do you think the student made these mistakes?

5   Grammar

1 You could explain the mistakes with the tenses in the composition above by contrasting some of the tenses. Read the explanations below, which contrast three tenses, and complete them.

The past simple tense and the past perfect tense

'When you're talking about states or actions that only took place in the
(a) .... and are now completely (b) .... , you (c) .... the past simple tense. You only use the past perfect (d) .... when there are two consecutive states or actions, and you want to stress that the (e) .... one happened before the other.'

The past simple tense and the past continuous tense

'When you want to talk about habitual or continuing (f) .... or states in the past you use the (g) .... simple tense or *used to*. You only use the past continuous tense for past actions or (h) .... that were (i) .... as something else happened, that is, for background actions or states.'

2 Would any of the following students find the above explanations helpful?
   a) A teenage intermediate student with a little formal knowledge of grammar.
   b) An adult intermediate student with a good formal knowledge of grammar.
   c) An adult intermediate student with no formal knowledge of grammar.

3 Talking points

Talk about one or both of the points below with a partner or partners.

• Are grammatical explanations helpful to students?

• Would you correct all the mistakes in the composition in Section 4 before returning it to the student? If not, which mistakes would you correct? Why? How would you correct them?

6   Writing: A letter

1 Read the last part of a letter you have recently received from an English teacher friend who is a student of Spanish.

> I'm thinking of giving up my course – I don't seem to be making any progress. I can't speak fluently or really understand radio or TV programmes. I don't know if I can wait six months before I go to Spain next year – I feel so discouraged now. What did you find helpful? If you've got any tips, I'd be glad to have them! Anyway, take care! Love Sandra

2 Write a letter replying to Sandra. Then exchange letters with a partner and ask and answer questions about your advice.

7   Reading

1 The pictures below illustrate the different stages of two consecutive language lessons. Look at them and, with a partner, work out what is going on in each picture.

2 Now read the passage below which describes the two lessons. Were you and your partner right?

   a) Each group gets into a closed circle and holds a conversation. This is recorded by passing the cassette recorder to each person as they speak. (The teacher remains outside the circle, but can be consulted by students if they need help.)
   b) The teacher plays the recording back to the group and students ask for unfamiliar words to be written up on the board. There are no further questions at this stage.
   c) The teacher asks the group to reflect on the conversation and pass comments on it.
   d) The teacher takes away the cassette and transcribes the conversation, marking errors with a simple system of notation.
   e) In the next lesson, students receive copies of the transcript and reflect on it for five minutes. They make their own corrections wherever possible.
   f) The recording is played through again and students ask questions about errors that they cannot correct themselves. During this stage, the teacher judges when to do a little spot remedial teaching and may also decide to devote a whole follow-up lesson to a particular point.
   g) Students receive copies of the cassette for private study, either at home or in a listening centre.

   The cycle begins again with a new conversation.

   (adapted from *C.L.L. (Community Language Learning) – A Way Forward?*: Rod Bolitho)

3 Look at the passage again. What is meant in (f) by:

   a) '*spot* remedial teaching'
   b) 'a *follow-up* lesson'?

4 Look at the list below. Match the verbs on the left with the nouns on the right. Some verbs may be matched with more than one noun.

   a) to get into   the teacher
   b) to hold   a recording
   c) to consult   a closed circle
   d) to play back   unfamiliar words
   e) to write up   remedial teaching
   f) to play through   a conversation
   g) to do

5 Now look at the pictures again and, without looking at the passage, describe to a partner what is happening in each stage of the lesson.

6 Talking points

Talk about one or both of the points below with a partner or partners.

- Do you think you could learn languages this way?

- Would you like to try teaching this way?

8 Classroom instructions: Introducing a conversation lesson

1 Imagine that a teacher has decided to try out for the first time the teaching technique described in Section 7 on page 19. The teacher might introduce the technique with the instructions below. Read them and then fill in the blanks.

'Right, now today we're going to do something (a) .... different from anything we've done before. It's a kind of conversation (b) .... OK?

'Now, I'm going to ask you to (c) .... into groups of six and I'm going to (d) .... each group a cassette recorder. Right, now, in your groups you're going to (e) .... a conversation and you're going to record what you say. OK? Now (f) .... you're talking I'll be here, walking around, and if there's anything you (g) .... to ask me, like how to say this or that, you just call me and I'll (h) .... and help. Now, what are you going to talk about? I'd like you to choose a topic from . . . '

2 Now introduce the same activity to a partner as if you were speaking to a class. Use your own words or those above.

9 Conclusions

1 Teaching-related vocabulary

In this unit there are many words and expressions related to teaching and learning. Read through the unit and write down ten items which you find particularly useful.

2 Reflections on teaching

- Look at the *Teaching/learning techniques* column in the chart opposite. Add two other techniques to this list.

  Do these techniques help you learn language? Complete the first column with your opinion.

Teaching/learning techniques	Your opinion	A's opinion	B's opinion
Listening to recordings of yourself			
Learning vocabulary lists by heart			
Studying the language at home with a friend			
Learning verb tables			
Doing pronunciation drills			
Listening to rapid conversations			

- Now fill in the other columns by finding out colleagues' opinions. Then discuss your answers.

3 About you

1 Starter activities

1 Look at the photographs of different schools. What do you think these schools are like (their students, teachers, atmosphere, buildings, etc.)?

Discuss your answers with a partner.

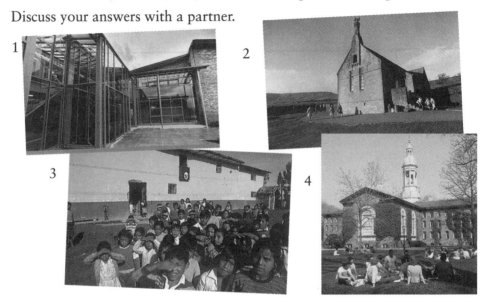

2 Are any of the schools in the photographs similar to the school where you work or where you were a student? Describe your school to a partner.

2 Reading

1 In the passage below George Finley, a teacher in his early forties, describes some of his experiences as a teacher. Read the passage through quickly. Then answer the question: Does George like teaching?

> I went into teaching for all the wrong reasons – short hours, long holidays and the idea that I'd have enough time to set up my own business. It didn't work out at all. I ought to have known better, as my father was a teacher, but he worked in a
> 5 grammar school. Although he brought marking home, his job was very different from mine, much more settled. It was easier for him to know what he was doing. If he saw my classroom, I'm sure he would be absolutely horrified. He just can't envisage what my school is like.

10   Before I became a teacher, I worked as a designer in industry. It was a dead-end job with no chance of making progress unless you were brilliant. So I went on a post-graduate teaching course for a year, which I enjoyed. It was much better than sitting in a factory working out pattern designs. I liked the academic side,

15   but the practical side wasn't very useful, though I understand it's much better now.

My first job was at a small primary school in an expensive dormitory village, very different from my present school. All the children were smartly dressed in uniform. They were expected

20   to move quietly from one classroom to another and to eat their lunch in total silence except for a short period of quiet chatting at the end. In assembly, the head stood behind a sort of lectern, in traditional fashion, with his staff ranged on either side. He once told the female staff, 'I like my ladies to wear skirts', and I

25   seem to remember that I was obliged to wear a collar and tie. In many ways he was running a nice little preparatory school which was what the parents wanted.

Although I liked the head personally, he reminded me of my father; I didn't feel that working in a school like that was doing

30   a lot for society. I wouldn't call myself a political – capital P – person, but I'd developed a bit of a social conscience by that time. So I left after two years.

After a while, I met up with a chap I'd worked with before, who was setting up a handicraft workshop. It seemed a good

35   idea so I threw in my lot with him, lost a lot of money and just avoided being made a bankrupt. When the business collapsed, I just wanted to get away. I'd met my present wife by then and we went abroad for four months. When we returned, I needed money desperately, so I went back to teaching.

40   I've been at this school for four years now. We have about three hundred pupils. The catchment area includes quite a large number of council houses and terraced houses like mine. The teaching is mainly informal, but staff are allowed to use their own methods. Unless things are going badly wrong, no one

45   interferes. We try to bring the children progressively towards a more secondary way of working. In the first year, they are with the class teacher almost constantly; but by the time they leave us at the age of twelve, they're moving around in groups from teacher to teacher.

50   The first two or three years in this school were very difficult for me, even though I'd already done quite a bit of teaching. The children didn't know how to act in a classroom situation: their socialisation wasn't complete. They couldn't sit at their desks and work, but wanted to make friends with the children

55   around them. There was a lot of talking and moving about. They weren't actually destroying the ceilings, but the relationship

deteriorated to such an extent that there was no way in which I
liked them and some of them disliked me.

It needs a lot of work to recover from that situation. A
60 teacher is very isolated. You can go to a colleague and say,
'They're a hell of a bunch', and get a sympathetic hearing,but
you've got to work it out for yourself ultimately. I overcame it
by trial and error. There's no prescription for getting control.
Maybe it's a shout or a threat or just waiting there with the right
65 expression on your face. There were times when none of these
worked. Teaching is an art, having an eye for the types of movements and an ear for the sounds that indicate the machine is not
running properly.

I like teaching much better now and I want to stay in this
70 school because I'm reaping the benefits of all the hard work I've
put into the relationship. I still have a yearning to set up another
business, though that will probably remain a dream. A lot of
teachers see their work as a vocation, but I could never feel
that. In some ways, I see myself as a performer, an entertainer,
75 setting up activities for the children at their level. If they enjoy
them, then the job is done.

(adapted from *Teachers*: Frank E. Hugget)

2 Read the passage again and complete, in note form, the chart below about
George. Then compare your answers with a partner.

Reasons for becoming a teacher	Short hours	Current teaching job	
Non-teaching jobs		Problems with teaching	
Teacher training		Pleasures from teaching	
First teaching job		Future plans	

3 Look at the list below of words and expressions from the passage. Explain
the meaning of each one to a partner as if you were talking to a group of
advanced students.

to work out (line 3)
to know better (line 4)
marking (line 5)
a dead-end job (line 11)
a post-graduate teaching course (line 12)
a dormitory village (line 18)

a uniform (line 19)
assembly (line 22)
a catchment area (line 41)
to deteriorate (line 57)
to reap the benefits (line 70)
a yearning (line 71)

4 Talking points

Talk about one or two of the points below with a partner or partners.

* Have you ever experienced problems like George's? If so, what techniques did you use to cope?

* Do you see yourself as 'a performer, an entertainer'?

* Do you see teaching as a vocation?

3 Grammar: The habitual past

1 Read sentences (a) and (b) below. Can *used to* and *would* be interchanged in these sentences? Could the past simple tense be used instead in these sentences?

a) I used to work in a primary school.
b) At the beginning of my teaching career I would spend hours and hours preparing lessons.

2 Read the grammar rules below. Are they true or false? If they are false, correct them.

a) *Used to* is used to contrast past habitual actions, states or situations with very remote past ones.
b) *Would*, when used to refer to the past, is only used for repeated past actions, not states or situations.

3 Tell a partner some of the things you used to do, or would do, in your early days as a teacher. If you are new to teaching, tell each other about what you used to do, or would do, as a pupil at primary school.

4 Speaking

1 Complete the chart about yourself in note form.

Reasons for becoming a teacher		Current teaching job	
Non-teaching jobs		Problems with teaching	
Teacher training		Pleasures from teaching	
First teaching job		Future plans	

2 Language functions

Read the expressions below and put them into three groups: *expressions of interest*, *expressions of sympathy* and *expressions of admiration*.

Really?	That sounds dreadful.
Did you?	That must have been really exciting.
I can imagine.	Right.
Were you?	Oh dear.
How awful.	That sounds wonderful.
How amazing!	That must have been horrible.

Now compare and discuss your answers to Activity 1 with a partner, using as many of the expressions above as you find appropriate.

5   Student language: Assessing oral communication

1 Listen to the conversation between two students: Alberto, who is Italian, and Maki, who is Japanese. They are carrying out a task their teacher has set them. What do you think the teacher has asked them to do?

2 Look at the list below of language learning difficulties. Which of these difficulties did (a) Alberto, and (b) Maki have? Which, if any, of these areas most aided or prevented their communication? Listen again to their conversation as many times as you like.

pronunciation
intonation
vocabulary
grammatical accuracy
fluency
other

6   Listening

1 Listen to four Irish women writers talking about their childhoods. Look at the chart below and tick the topics each person mentions.

	Clare Boylan	Edna O'Brien	Dervla Murphy	Maeve Binchy
Their home environment	✓			
Their first memory				
Their family				
Their relationship with others				
Their toys and pastimes				

2 Listen again and note down the important points each speaker makes. Then compare your answers with a partner.

3 Talking point

• Tell a partner about the same aspects of your own childhood.

7   Writing: An autobiography

Write a short autobiography (about 250 words). Include any information which you think others will find interesting.

Then display it for others to read. Read the others' autobiographies and discuss them.

8 Classroom instructions: Introducing a reading activity

1 A teacher might introduce Section 2, Activity 1 on page 22, with the instructions below. Read them and then fill in the blanks.

> 'Right, now we're going to move (*a*) .... to something different. We're going to read a (*b*) .... in which a teacher talks about his experiences as a teacher. Now the first time you read it, I'd like you to read it fairly quickly and don't (*c*) .... attention to the details of the passage or worry (*d*) .... any words you don't understand – we'll come (*e*) .... to them later. OK? Right, now, I just want you to read it (*f*) .... quickly and answer the question – I'll write it (*g*) .... the board. . . .
>
> 'OK. Are you clear (*h*) .... what you're going to do? Could someone explain (*i*) .... us please? Takako? . . . OK, fine, thanks, yes, that's right.
>
> 'Now, the passage starts (*j*) .... page 22. So, could you find it, please? Everybody OK? OK, can you start reading?'

2 Now introduce the same activity to a partner as if you were speaking to a class. Use your own words or those above.

9 Conclusions

1 Teaching-related vocabulary

Look at the headings below. List under each heading four or five words which describe your own school or college. Then compare and discuss your answers with a partner.

School buildings   *School activities*
School atmosphere   *School teaching style*

2 Reflections on teaching

- Have you enjoyed talking about yourself in this unit? Why? Why not?

- In what ways can it be helpful to learning to bring students' experiences and feelings into the classroom?

- Can personalisation of this kind ever be harmful in the classroom?

- What do you do to personalise your lessons?

4 Talking about coursebooks

1 Starter activities

1 List the names of all the EFL coursebooks you can think of.

2 Read the excerpts from some reviews of EFL coursebooks below. Write next to each one the name of a coursebook it reminds you of.

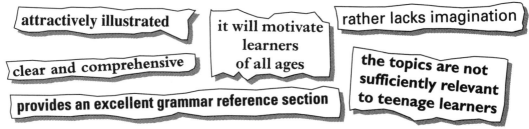

attractively illustrated

it will motivate learners of all ages

rather lacks imagination

clear and comprehensive

provides an excellent grammar reference section

the topics are not sufficiently relevant to teenage learners

3 Complete this sentence:

My favourite English coursebook is .... because ....

Then compare and discuss your answers to Activities 1–3 with a partner.

2 Listening

1 You are going to listen to three teachers of English discussing the coursebooks they learnt English from at school. The teachers are German and are in their thirties. What do you imagine their coursebooks were like? Listen to the conversation to see if you guessed correctly.

2 Listen again and complete the chart below in note form. Then compare and discuss your answers with a partner.

What their books contained	What their books didn't contain	What they learnt at school	What they didn't learn at school
Texts			

3 The words below are all from the conversation. Put a dot (•) above the main stressed syllable in each word.

a) coursebook   i)   interaction
b) problem   j)   synonym
c) grammar   k)   definition
d) exercise   l)   opposite
e) communicative   m) cassette
f) activity   n)   situation
g) dialogue
h) conversation

Now check your answers with the cassette. Then repeat the words.

4 Talking points

Talk about one or both of the points below with a partner or partners.

• Do the coursebooks these German teachers describe seem good to you?

• Describe the coursebook(s) you learnt English from.

3   Grammar: The past simple tense and the present perfect tense

1 Complete the sentences with the correct tense (past simple or present perfect) of the verb in brackets.

a) The coursebook I .... (use) when I learnt English was very interesting.

b) We .... (teach) with the same coursebook for years now. It's so good.

c) Since I started teaching, I .... (never ask) my students to translate in class.

d) When I first visited England I .... (not understand) anything anyone said to me.

e) When I was a student my teacher often .... (ask) us to do grammar exercises.

f) We never once .... (speak) English in class when I was at school.

g) From the moment I started teaching I .... (always believe) it is very important for students to speak English in class.

h) In the last fifteen years or so the spoken language .... (become) more important than the written language. That .... (not be) the case before.

2 Are these sentences true or false? Write T (true) or F (false) next to each one. Correct the false ones.

 a) The past simple tense is used for states or actions that have no connection with the present.
 b) The present perfect tense is used for states or actions that began in the past and have already finished.

4   Reading

1 What is the purpose of the questionnaire below? Read it through quickly to find out.

CHOOSING A TEXTBOOK

Does the book suit your students?

I	Is it attractive? Given the average age of your students, would they enjoy using it?	YES	PARTLY	NO
2	Is it culturally acceptable?	YES	PARTLY	NO
3	Does it reflect what you know about your students' needs and interests?	YES	PARTLY	NO
4	Is it about the right level of difficulty?	YES	PARTLY	NO
5	Is it about the right length?	YES	PARTLY	NO
6	Are the course's physical characteristics appropriate? (e.g. is it durable?)	YES	PARTLY	NO
7	Are there enough authentic materials, so that the students can see that the book is relevant to real life?	YES	PARTLY	NO
8	Does it achieve an acceptable balance between *knowledge about* the language, and *practice in using* the language?	YES	PARTLY	NO
9	Does it achieve an acceptable balance between the relevant language skills, and integrate them so that work in one skill area helps the others?	YES	PARTLY	NO
10	Does the book contain enough communicative activities to enable the students to use the language independently?	YES	PARTLY	NO

Does the book suit the teacher?

I	Is your overall impression of the contents and layout of the course favourable?	YES	PARTLY	NO
2	Is there a good, clear teacher's guide with answers and help on methods and additional activities?	YES	PARTLY	NO

↓

---

3 Can one use the book in the classroom without constantly having to turn to the teacher's guide?	YES	PARTLY	NO
4 Are the recommended methods and approaches suitable for you, your students and your classroom?	YES	PARTLY	NO
5 Are the approaches easily adaptable if necessary?	YES	PARTLY	NO
6 Does the course require little or no time-consuming preparation?	YES	PARTLY	NO
7 Are useful ancillary materials such as tapes, workbooks, and visuals provided?	YES	PARTLY	NO
8 Is there sufficient provision made for tests and revision?	YES	PARTLY	NO
9 Does the book use a 'spiral' approach, so that items are regularly revised and used again in different contexts?	YES	PARTLY	NO
10 Is the course appropriate for, and liked by, colleagues?	YES	PARTLY	NO

Does the book suit the syllabus and examination?

1 Has the book been recommended or approved by the authorities?	YES	PARTLY	NO
2 Does the book follow the official syllabus in a creative manner?	YES	PARTLY	NO
3 Is the course well-graded, so that it gives well-structured and systematic coverage of the language?	YES	PARTLY	NO
4 If it does more than the syllabus requires, is the result an improvement?	YES	PARTLY	NO
5 Are the activities, contents and methods used in the course well-planned and executed?	YES	PARTLY	NO
6 Has it been prepared specifically for the target examination?	YES	PARTLY	NO
7 Do the course's methods help the students prepare for the exam?	YES	PARTLY	NO
8 Is there a good balance between what the examination requires, and what the students need?	YES	PARTLY	NO
9 Is there enough examination practice?	YES	PARTLY	NO
10 Does the course contain useful hints on examination technique?	YES	PARTLY	NO

(from *Making the Most of Your Textbook*: Neville Grant)

2 Read the questionnaire again and answer the questions with reference to a coursebook which you are currently using or which you know well. Then compare your answers with a partner.

3 Were the words listed below in the questionnaire? Without reading the questionnaire again, underline the words you think were in it.

syllabus	grammar	layout
vocabulary	systematic	grading
artwork	user-friendly	suited
type size	attractive	coverage
balance	comprehensive	relevance
skills	lessons	texts

Now check your answers.

4 The words in the chart below are all derived from words in the questionnaire. Complete the chart where possible.

Verb	Noun	Positive adjective	Negative adjective
to suit	suitability		
		attractive	
		acceptable	
-------			inappropriate
-------	relevance		
to balance			
	use		
to adapt			
			ungraded
		(well) structured	

6 Speaking

1 The list below includes some factors to consider when choosing a coursebook for a class. Read it and add any factors that you think are missing. Then number the factors in order of importance (1 = most important, 7 = least important).

topics which will engage students' interest	right level
communicative activities	clear teacher's guide
comprehensive coverage of syllabus	systematic approach
attractive presentation	

4 Language functions

What do the expressions below have in common? Read them and then complete the heading.

Ways of changing the . . . .

Anyway, . . .	Something else . . .
Sorry, but . . .	That reminds me of . . .
By the way . . .	Another point . . .
I'd just like to say something else . . .	Besides that, . . .

3 Now discuss your answers to Activity 1 with a partner. In your discussion, use the expressions above where appropriate.

7 Student language: Assessing written work

Read the poster and the two letters from students entering this competition. Which one would you give the prize to? Why?

> # WIN A PRIZE
>
> ## WOULD YOU LIKE TO WIN:
> ## AN ENGLISH–ENGLISH DICTIONARY
> ## OR
> ## AN ENGLISH GRAMMAR BOOK
> ## OR
> ## A SET OF ENGLISH LANGUAGE CASSETTES?
>
> Just write a letter to your teacher
> explaining which prize you'd like
> to win and why.
>
> The best letter wins the prize.

Dear Shân

I would like to win an English-English dictionary. I bought an English-Deutsch dictionary about 3 months ago in Switzerland and I thought it was useful for me but I understand now that it's much better an English-English one.

You told us one day about the dictionary and you said that is more complete so we can learn better the language with this book. I was checking in the library but it was too expensive. So I hope to win it. I think it can be useful when I watch TV, when I go to the cinema, when I read a book etc.

I like dictionary with a lot of pictures. So I can quickly understand the meaning of the words.

Best wishes Laurence

Dear Shân

In this competition I'd like to win a set of english language learning cassette tapes, because my accent is very bad. Do you know this, don't you?

I think if I won this prize I could practice a lot and improve my english.

You know how important it is for me.

But I have another reason why I want to win this prize. In Portugal I can watch satellite TV and I need to understand when I listen. In my country I have had good films in English channel and I haven't understood, but now if I win this prize I won't have any problems more.

I think this prize could help me.

If I won this prize, I'd listen to the tapes 8 hours a day because I'm a busy man and I think the best way to learn English is when I am sleeping.

Best Wishes
José Carlos P. Carvajino

8 Writing: A book review

1 Look at the list of functions and match them with the expressions:

Functions	*Expressions*
a) to conclude	on the one hand . . . on the other
b) to sequence ideas	as far as X is concerned
c) to make contrasts	next
d) to refer to things	in conclusion
e) to join points together	both . . . and
	firstly
	last of all
	with regard to X
	finally
	however
	not only . . . but also
	lastly

2 Write a review for your colleagues of a coursebook they may not know. Write it so as to help them decide whether they should use it or not. Use some of the expressions above, if appropriate, and refer to the questionnaire on pages 31–2 for points to consider. Then display your review where your colleagues can read it.

9   Classroom instructions: Introducing a writing activity

1 A teacher might introduce Section 8, Activity 2 on page 35 with the following instructions. Read them and then fill in the blanks.

> 'OK, now I'd like (*a*) .... to move on to (*b*) .... some writing. What I'd like you to do is write a review of a coursebook you know well. And I'd like you to imagine that your partners are the people you're writing the review (*c*) .... Because after you've written your reviews I'd like you to (*d*) .... them up on the wall – somewhere where everyone can read them, (*e*) .... you'll be able to (*f*) .... an idea about what some coursebooks are like.
>
> 'OK? Is that (*g*) .... ? You're going to write a review of a coursebook and (*h*) .... display it (*i*) .... the wall where everyone else'll be able to read it. If you want to, you can (*j*) .... back to the questionnaire on pages 31 and 32 for ideas.'

2 Now introduce the same activity to a partner as if you were speaking to a class. Use your own words or those above.

10   Conclusions

1 Teaching-related vocabulary

Read through the unit and list as many vocabulary items as you can under these three headings:

Teaching aids   Teaching/learning activities   Syllabus

2 Reflections on teaching

Imagine what your ideal coursebook would be like, and then write five statements about it in large bubbles. Display your bubbles and compare and discuss them with a partner.

5   Talking about lessons

1   Starter activities

1 Look at the photographs. Describe what you can see and discuss what kind of lessons they seem to be.

1   2

3   4

2 What do you think creates a successful lesson? Look at the list below and number the various factors in order of importance (1 = most important, 6 = least important). Then discuss your answers with a partner.

good lesson planning
the teacher's knowledge of the subject
the relationship between the teacher
   and the students

the students' interest in the
   subject
the appropriate teaching method
other (specify)

2   Reading

1 Look at the headlines below. What do they suggest the article is about?

Teaching with a magic touch

Karen Gold learns that a pat on the back brings the best out of the class

A PAT on the back is worth a dozen curricular innovations, according to a study of how teachers touch their pupils in primary schools.

When teachers supplement praise with a pat, the whole class works on average 20 per cent harder, say researchers looking at 16 West Midlands primary schools.

In one class children concentrated almost twice as hard when their teacher added a touch to every 'Well done'; in another, bad behaviour fell by more than two thirds after the teacher combined a pat with praise.

Touch studies were the brainchild of Kate Bevan, an education lecturer at Wolverhampton Polytechnic. She and two Birmingham University researchers spent more than 50 hours in 16 classes, watching children aged four to six and categorising how often teachers touched their pupils, when, where and why.

Almost none of the teachers used touch to accompany praise. Mostly they touched the head, shoulder, hand, arm or back to move a child to

another part of the classroom, show it how to do something – hold a pencil, for example – or for no apparent reason.

The researchers' theory was that a touch would reinforce praise. So, without telling the teachers what they were investigating, they asked four of those previously observed to stop all touching *except* when praising their pupils. They should touch whenever they praised, but they should not praise more than usual.

The results were staggering. Children's normal concentration in different classes ranged from 75 per cent of the three-minute spells of observation to only 39 per cent of the time. But during the praise-touch weeks, concentration in every class soared: to more than 90 per cent of the time in the harder-working classes; to 69 per cent of the time – almost double – in the ones where children had worked properly less than half the day.

The teachers achieved this without any extra praise, and with fewer pats over all, because all the incon-

sequential touches stopped. They kept control without touching, too: in the two classes where disruption as well as concentration was measured, incidents such as water throwing and pencil-grabbing fell by almost two-thirds.

The teachers were amazed. 'Some of them weren't even aware that they touched children at all,' says Kate Bevan. 'None of them had any idea it would have such a potent effect.'

She believes that a pat reinforced the pleasure of being praised, particularly for young children who are still more familiar with actions than words. Praise then becomes more memorable for the touched child and those nearby.

Touch is not on the teacher-training curriculum. Kate Bevan, who trains teachers, believes it should be: 'Teachers can only do what they feel comfortable with, but this is part of the teacher's answer to what makes children work hard and what motivates them. They should at least be aware of it.'

(from *The Independent on Sunday*)

2 Read the article to check your answer to Activity 1. Which of the factors listed in Section 1, Activity 2 is important, according to the article?

3 Complete the short summary of the article.

> Some researchers initially (*a*) .... how often teachers touched their pupils. They then (*b*) .... the teachers to touch their pupils (*c*) .... when they praised them. They found that in the classes in which teachers touched (*d*) .... they praised, the pupils' (*e*) .... increased dramatically and disruption in the class (*f*) ....

4 Why, according to the article, does patting have such an effect?

5 Look at the list below of words and expressions from or based on the article. Put a tick next to those which you might use to talk about a lesson you enjoyed, and a cross next to those you might use to refer to a lesson you found difficult. Then compare your answers with a partner.

concentrate	pencil-grabbing
disruption	bad behaviour
water-throwing	hard-working
praise	Well done!

6 Talking points

Talk about one or two of the points below with a partner or partners.

- What do you think about the results of this experiment?

- Do you think patting would have the same effect with secondary age or adult students?

- Do/Would you pat your students? Why/Why not?

3 Grammar: The present perfect and the present perfect continuous tenses

1 Look at the two groups of sentences. All six sentences include verbs in the present perfect tense, but each group expresses a different use of this tense. What are these different uses?

Group 1: Have you ever patted your students?
     She has had problems in concentrating.
     He has done some classroom research.

Group 2: He has worked well this term.
     She hasn't been off school once this term.
     The new teacher has had a lot to cope with this week.

2 Now look at the three pairs of sentences below. Each pair includes one verb in the present perfect tense and one in the present perfect continuous tense. What is the difference between the two tenses?

I have been teaching all day.
I have taught all my working life.

He has been having problems with concentration.
He has had problems with concentration since he joined the school.

She has been behaving badly.
She has behaved badly.

3 Describe to a partner what you have been doing with your classes this term and what kind of work you have done since you started teaching.

4   Student language: Assessing written work

1 Read the assessment of a lesson below, written by a student. What kind of activities does this student seem to like?

---

1. What you liked about the lesson and why.

I made an interview, (with another boy); we have chosen some questions and after, with a cassette recorder, we have interviewed some teachers of our school! Then We have done a trascription. Good, very Good exercise for, writing, listening and speaking too (with my frend but, in particular with English people or teachers.)

2. What you disliked about the lesson and why.

About this lesson, nothing!
About others lessons, sometime too much stupid plays! with the children, it's a good idea to teach english with plays but with the adults, it's often a waste of time! It's possible to spend better our time.

3. What you learnt from the lesson.

I understood that is very important to improve my listening because it's so different the english to spoke from by English people rather then than english spoke by foreigners.   I learnt , new words, expressions.

4. What you are still unsure about from the lesson.

I

5. What your study plans are before the next lesson and for the next lesson.

usually I try to look over (to pass again) the last lesson

---

2 Where, in your opinion, is this student's most serious language mistake? In Answer 1, 2, 3 or 5? Why?

3 If you were this student's teacher, would you correct the mistakes in Answers 1, 2, 3 or 5? Why/Why not?

5   Listening

1 You are going to listen to three teachers discussing what makes a good lesson. Look at the list of possible factors below, and then listen. Put a tick next to those they mention.

A good lesson . . .
a) is fun.
b) includes games.
c) has a varied pace.
d) gives students a sense of achievement.
e) matches the students' expectations.

f) makes students feel involved.
g) follows methods the students are used to.
h) has a wide range of activities.
i) has clear goals for the students.
j) doesn't depart from the teacher's lesson plan.

2 Language functions

Look at the list below of functions performed by the people holding the conversation. Listen again and write down the language the speakers used for each function. Then compare your answers with a partner.

a) introducing an idea/topic
b) drawing conclusions

c) agreeing with someone
d) clarifying/expanding on something

Now practise saying some of the expressions aloud.

3 The expressions in the list below are all taken from or based on the conversation. Read the list and put a tick next to those items which occurred or which were present in your last lesson. Then compare your answers with a partner.

a) an element of fun
b) variety of pace
c) quiet moments

d) working as a whole class
e) a sense of achievement
f) clear goals

6   Speaking

Look at the ten statements in Section 5, Activity 1. Put a tick next to those you agree with and a cross next to those you disagree with. Add in any factors you think are missing.

Then discuss your opinions with a partner, using the language you noted down in Section 5, Activity 2 where appropriate. Ask another person to listen to your discussion and note down which, if any, of these functions you and your partner use.

7 Writing: A description of a lesson

The three articles below all describe 'Lessons that have worked', and were written by Portuguese teachers of English for a magazine series. Read the articles and discuss them with a partner. Would you like to teach these lessons? Why/Why not?

Then write about a lesson of yours that has 'worked' and display your description where your colleagues can read it.

ABOUT ENGLAND
George Hayes
Esc. Preparatória de Lagoa
São Miguel

I decided that I wanted my pupils to learn something about England, so for the first half of the class I showed them slides with views of England. Then for the last part of the class I gave them some magazines with lots of pictures to look at. During all this time I had the tape recorder playing typical English music softly as a background. It was a great success and they all enjoyed it very much.

DESCRIBING PEOPLE – GAMES AND ACTIVITIES
Fátima Beatriz Lopes
São Miguel

1. I was teaching 'Describing People'

I went out of the room while the pupils chose one from among them. Then I came in and asked them: 'Has he got brown eyes?', 'Is he tall?' . . . When I got all the information about the pupil I guessed his name. Then I repeated the game with other children. And I think it worked out.
   Another way of doing this is for the child whose name has been guessed to leave the room. Then after coming back s/he has to guess the next pupil. This provides extra question practice.

(from *The British Council Newsletter for Portuguese Teachers of English*)

ROLE PLAYS
Maria de Fátima Aráujo
São Miguel, Azores

Every time I find some subject difficult for my pupils, I decide to do a role play, so that they can be interested in what's going on in the classroom.
   A role play which worked out very well was one about 'shopping'. The students were all volunteers and they had to come to the front of the classroom to do the acting.
   At the beginning they were quite shy and embarrassed (all they wanted to do was go back to their places) but the moment the first pair started talking they forgot all the embarrassment and they were quite at ease. When they finished the acting I praised them.
   The other pupils in the classroom, who had been watching the scene, were very anxious to do the same as their colleagues had done. So they took the initiative and asked me if they could act. As my answer was affirmative they started. The second pair was, of course, better than the first because they were no longer afraid of their colleagues' opinions.
   At the end of the class the pupils were very proud of their acting — they had done something different and they were proud of it.
   This is the trick I always use when I realise pupils are not interested in the class, and this trick always works. Children like playing roles and pretending they are someone else. This is an opportunity they have to be creative and to enter a world of imagination and fantasy – a world of their own.

---

8 Classroom instructions: Preparing for a speaking activity

1 A teacher might introduce Section 6 on page 41 with the instructions below. Read them and then fill in the blanks.

'OK, can you stop what you're doing? Right, we're going to go (*a*) .... to something else – some speaking practice. Can you look at Section 5, Activity 1 on page 41 (*b*) .... your books? Got it? Now in that activity, there are ten statements, all about what makes a good lesson. Do you agree (*c*) .... these statements? Wait a minute, hold (*d*) .... a minute. If you agree with the statements, I want (*e*) .... to tick them. If you don't agree, what do you think you should do? Yes, that's right, put a (*f*) .... next to them. OK, so do you understand what you've (*g*) .... to do? Read the statements and tick the (*h*) .... you agree with and put a cross next to the ones you disagree with. OK, off you go.'

2 Now introduce the same activity to a partner as if you were speaking to a class. Use your own words or those above. Then continue the instructions.

9 Conclusions

1 Teaching-related vocabulary

Find five classroom activities mentioned in this unit that are relevant to your teaching situation. Discuss your answers with a partner.

2 Reflections on teaching

Look at the list below of some of the activities in this unit. Discuss with a partner which ones you preferred and why. Do you think your students would feel the same as you?

Gap-filling to check comprehension of a reading passage (Section 2, Activity 3)
Discussing a topic in order to use target language (Section 3, Activity 3)
Identifying a student's mistakes (Section 4, Activity 2)
Listening for specific information (Section 5, Activity 1)
Writing about something you have done and displaying it for others to read (Section 7)

6 Talking about relationships

1 Starter activities

1 Look at the animals below. Which animal(s) do you think a teacher should be like in his/her school relationships? If none of them seem appropriate, draw a picture of a suitable one on a piece of paper. Then discuss your views with a partner.

2 What animal are you like in your relationships with your:

a) students?
b) colleagues?
c) headteacher or director?

Discuss your answers with a partner.

2 Listening

1 You are going to listen to a British teacher talking about some of her professional relationships. Look at the list of people below and then listen. Put a tick next to those she mentions.

pupils/children headmaster
colleagues   friends
school assistants administrators
parents   education authorities
classes   school inspectors

2 Listen again and note down the main point the teacher makes about each person or group of people.

3 Look at the list below of adjectives used by the teacher. Who is she describing with each one?

a) fatherly   d) safe
b) tough   e) ashamed
c) strict   f) inadequate

Do any of these words describe you or some of the people you work with? Discuss your answers with a partner.

4 Talking points

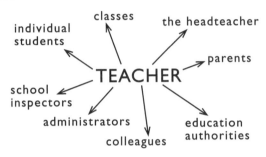

Look at the diagram and talk about one or both of the points below with a partner or partners.

• Which of the relationships do you value most? Why?

• What contribution can your relationship with each of these individuals or groups make to your teaching?

3 Grammar: Relative clauses

1 Read the sentences about the teacher in the listening passage. Complete them with *that, who* or *whom*. You may be able to use more than one of these pronouns in a gap. In some sentences you may not need any of them; in this case, write —. Then compare and discuss your answers with a partner.

a) The inspector .... was called by the headmaster couldn't control the class.
b) The headmaster .... worked at her first school didn't like her.
c) The class .... the inspector tried to teach laughed at him.

d) The children with .... she worked at first were very tough.
e) Parents, ... often wish to know what is happening, are welcome to help her in class.
f) Parents .... help with reading are not allowed to teach.
g) She gets angry about teachers .... just do the absolute minimum.
h) Some parents .... the teacher expected to volunteer didn't do so.

2 Match the explanations below with the sentences in Activity 1.

(i)   You can omit *who* or *that* in this sentence because it is not the subject of a verb.
(ii) You cannot use *that* in this sentence because *that* cannot be used in non-defining clauses.
(iii) You can use *who* or *that* in defining clauses, so both are possible answers in this sentence.
(iv) You can use *who* or *whom* in this sentence. They can both be used after a preposition.

3 Use the chart to write six sentences about your own teaching situation. For example:

The teachers (who(m)) I work with are great.

The teachers with whom I work are great.

The	teachers headteacher class	(preposition)	who whom that ———	. . .

Then compare and discuss your answers with a partner.

4 Speaking

1 Imagine that at the beginning of term, six students in one of your classes cannot decide where to sit this term. Read about them and the classroom and then decide where they should sit.

THE CLASSROOM

The desks are grouped as follows. Those marked with an X are empty.

```
                                    ┌──┐  Teacher's desk
                                    └──┘
                               X    X
 __   __      __   __          __   __

 __   __      __   __          __   __

 __   __      __   __          __   __

 X    X       X    X           __   __
```

THE STUDENTS

Martin: a very bright student who lacks concentration and spends a lot of his time unintentionally disturbing others.
Maria: a very serious student who does not relate well to her classmates. She is withdrawn and lacks self-confidence.
Richard: an easy-going student who works well when he chooses to.
Sara: a sociable student who gets on well with others. Sara likes school and school work but her serious problems at home depress her.
David: a keen and well-disposed student but one who has great difficulty in learning. Others tend to laugh at him.
Anna: a well-balanced character who is generally a good student.

2 Language functions

Sometimes you want to bring people into a conversation by inviting them to give their opinion. Some expressions for doing so are listed below. Read them and then discuss your decisions in Activity 1, using as many of the expressions as you find appropriate.

What/How about you, (Maria)?	Would you go along with that?
What do you think?	How does that strike you?
Would you agree with that?	How does that sound?
What's your opinion, (Maria)?	

5   Reading

1 These five texts all have one thing in common. What is it? Read them and find out.

1 I'm 14 and very unhappy. When I was 7 my parents got divorced and my Dad went to live about 50 miles away. My mum started drinking and now she drinks all the time. Sometimes she doesn't cook us anything or clean the house.

My two older brothers have started drinking now too, and have started hitting me a lot. My mum doesn't take any notice of them – I don't know what to do. Please tell me how I can get out of this awful situation.

2 I'm happily married, with two grown-up children and four grandchildren. However I have been feeling lately as if I can't cope with my family any more. I work part-time, but they still expect me to do a lot for them. My father lives nearby and, as he suffers from arthritis, needs a lot of care and attention. My daughter's got five-month-old twins and asks me to help her with them quite often. And my husband is finding his work very stressful at the moment and needs a lot of support from me. The problem is I just can't look after them all and so feel guilty and a failure. How can I help them without making myself ill?

3

My Dad

Gary Sharpe (aged 15)

My Dad and I go out together,
We watch the football despite the weather.
We shout and cheer and both agree
That Tottenham are the best to see.

I feel my Dad is getting old,
He's fat and bald and feels the cold,
And when he dances it's such a giggle,
His feet don't move but he gives a wiggle.

I don't much like his taste in clothes,
He's hardly with it as fashion goes.
But somehow I feel he is my mate,
In fact I think my Dad is great.

The time has come for me to admit,
That my Dad to me is quite a hit.
I wouldn't swop him for any other -
Apart from which he's married to my Mother.

4

My Mum

Kim Voller (aged 14)

My Mum has dyed auburn hair,
It's hard to believe she once was fair.
She has her hair set every Sunday,
But it's always flat again by Monday.

She's always washing, ironing, cleaning
Until the house is really gleaming.
She gets up at five - that's her rule -
And gets us all up for work and school.

I shout at her and make her blue,
But I still love her, that is true.
I love her with all my heart,
And I hope that we will never part.

(ibid.)

(from *Preludes: Families*, Heinemann Educational, 1971)

48

5

PEOPLE ARE LIKE THAT

A romantic interlude by Marisa Arnold

A girl is waiting for her boyfriend...

G. At last you've come. I've been waiting for you for almost an hour.

B. I'm sorry, but it wasn't my fault. There was the traffic and...

G. Always the same excuse. On Tuesday, I was waiting for you from eight till half past nine.

B. I've already explained. The car suddenly stopped and I had to call my reliable mechanic.

G. Is your mechanic a nice blonde girl?

B. A nice blonde girl? Why are you saying such a thing? You know him.

G. Yes, I know him. That's why I was somewhat surprised when Lucy told me she had seen you in your car with a girl whose description reminded me of your secretary.

B. Try to calm yourself. Why don't you believe me? Don't you trust me? You know how much I love you. I could never lie to you for anything in the world. I would do anything to make you happy. Lucy has surely mistaken another person for me. When I finish work I'm already looking forward to seeing you. I'm not interested in other girls. You're the only one in my life.

G. Apart from the one who leaves lipstick on your cheek and even on your shirt collar?

B. What?

G. Lipstick. I told you. Tuesday, on your collar.

B. Strange. That's odd...

(from *Fun Press*, the magazine of student work from the British Council, Naples)

2 Look at the words for feelings in the circle. Which feelings are expressed in each text in Activity 1?

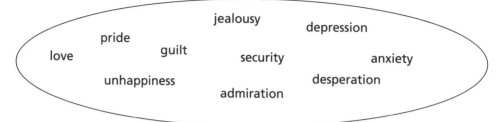

jealousy

depression

pride

guilt

love

security

anxiety

unhappiness

desperation

admiration

3 How do you think the situations described in the texts should/will develop?

4 Talking points

Talk about one or both of the points below with a partner or partners.

- What feelings do you experience or see others (teachers, students, directors/headteachers, administrators) expressing most often at school?
- Do any of these feelings worry you? How do you deal with them?

6 Student language: Assessing oral communication

1 Which of the relationships listed below are most important to you? Number them in order of importance (1 = most important, 5 = least important).

parents   neighbours
boy/girlfriend   other members of your family
friends

2 Two students – a Turkish woman and a Saudi Arabian man – were asked to do the same activity. Listen to an extract from their conversation and complete the chart with their opinions.

Relationship	Female student	Male student
Parents		1
Boyfriend/girlfriend		
Friends		
Neighbours		
Other members of your family		

3 Now complete the chart below with your views of the two students' language level (1 = very good, 2 = good, 3 = weak).

	Female student	*Male student*
Pronunciation		
Vocabulary		
Grammatical accuracy		
Fluency		
Communication		

4 Talking points

Talk about one or both of the points below with a partner or partners.

- Do you agree with the students' opinions?
- The male student contributes more to the conversation than the female student. Do you think this is due to his level of language, his gender, his personality or anything else?

7 Writing: A letter to a new class

1 At the beginning of term some teachers write a letter to everyone in their class.* In this letter they may outline their teaching aims and style, their interests, their family life, etc. The aim is to establish a private channel of communication with each individual student in the class. Each student can then choose to use or not to use this as he/she wants. It can develop into a regular exchange of letters between the teacher and individuals.

Choose a class of yours and write the first letter you might write to them. Then display your letter and read other people's. Discuss them.

2 What do you think of this idea of exchanging letters between the teacher and individuals in a class?

* (following an idea of Herbert R. Kohl)

8 Classroom instructions: Giving instructions for homework

1 A teacher might set part of Section 5 on pages 48–50 as homework with the instructions below. Read them and then fill in the blanks.

'Right, I'd like to give you some homework. We've done a lot of listening and speaking today but we haven't done much reading, so (a) .... like you to do some reading. It's the texts and tasks (b) .... pages 48 and 49 of your books. Can you look at them now? Just read the exercises through to (c) .... sure you know what you have to do. OK? Now (d) .... Activity 1 just write a very short answer; for Activity 2 just write the word for the feeling (e) .... the number of the text and for Activity 3 write me a paragraph (f) .... each situation. OK? Is this clear? Manuel, could you explain the homework to (g) .... ?
'Thank you. Now, could you do the homework on a (h) .... of paper and get it in to me (i) .... Friday. OK?'

2 Now introduce the same activity to a partner as if you were speaking to a class. Use your own words or those above.

9 Conclusions

1 Teaching-related vocabulary

The words and expressions below are related to relationships and are from this unit. Give an opposite for each item. Then compare and discuss your answers with a partner.

a) to give in to someone/something
b) to be involved in something
c) strict
d) to get on well with someone
e) security
f) pride
g) to laugh at someone/something
h) anxiety

2 Reflections on teaching

Spend a few minutes thinking about a relationship at school that you find positive and/or supportive and another relationship which worries you. How can you develop these relationships?

7 Teacher development

1 Starter activities

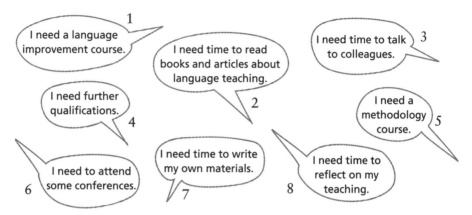

1 I need a language improvement course.

2 I need time to read books and articles about language teaching.

3 I need time to talk to colleagues.

4 I need further qualifications.

5 I need a methodology course.

6 I need to attend some conferences.

7 I need time to write my own materials.

8 I need time to reflect on my teaching.

1 The quotations above are from teachers who are saying what they need to help them with their teaching. Read them and put a tick next to the ones which are true for you. Add other statements if you wish. Then compare your answers with a partner.

2 Look at the cartoon below and imagine that the person in it is a teacher. What do you think the cartoonist is trying to say? Discuss your answers with a partner.

2   Reading

1 The article below by Alan Maley makes a distinction between teacher training (TT) and teacher development (TD). Read it and decide if the needs expressed by the teachers in Section 1 are TT or TD. Write the appropriate letters beside each quotation.

Teacher Development Explained

The Teacher Development (TD) movement is a relatively recent phenomenon. How has the need for TD arisen? There are at least five overlapping reasons:

- A feeling that training courses cannot alone satisfy all trainees' needs.
- A need to go beyond mere training. ('Is there a life after the course?')
- The search for a sense of direction which characterises the increasing professionalisation of ELT.
- The growing confidence of teachers in their ability to shape their own growth.
- The influence of the wider life-long education movement.

TD v Teacher Training
Explicitly or implicitly TD is often compared with Teacher Training (TT). Such comparisons certainly help to clarify the respective merits of TD and TT:

Teacher Training	Teacher Development
• time-bound	• continuing
• related to needs of course	• related to needs of the individual
• terminal outcomes pre-empted	• terminal outcomes open
• information/skills transmission	• problem solving
• fixed agenda	• flexible agenda
• hierarchical	• peer-oriented
• other-directed	• inner-directed
• top-down	• bottom-up

The single characteristic which crucially distinguishes TD is the vesting of decision making in teachers rather than in organisations, however well-intentioned. In TD it is the **teacher** who decides **whether** to undertake a given project, **which one, who with, how, where, when, how often, for how long** – and **why**, and who bears the responsibility for these decisions.

What is TD?
Since no single definition will suffice, examples may help to characterise a 'family resemblance'.

1. Teacher A feels constantly under stress, is sleeping badly and is off her food. She decides to act. After reading articles/books on stress and on personal organisation, she decides to set aside 30 minutes 'quiet time' daily and to use this to make lists of personal action points.
2. Teacher B finds a good practical idea in *P.E.T.*! He decides, with a colleague, to try it out for a month and to discuss progress once a week.
3. Ten teachers from School X decide to meet once a month to discuss a book or article all have agreed to read.
4. Eight teachers from School Y decide to meet once a month to talk over problems individuals have encountered. There is no agenda but the group is tolerant and mutually supportive.
5. Teacher C decides to take a course on a non-ELT subject, which she thinks may give new insights for her teaching. (For example, a course on counselling skills, Neuro-Linguistic Programming, photography, and so on.)
6. Teacher D decides to improve his qualifications. He enrols on a RSA Dip. TEFL course.
7. Teacher E has never written for a publication. She decides to review a recent book she feels enthusiastic about. She seeks advice from more experienced colleagues on how to write it and who to submit it to.
8. Teachers G and H decide to implement ideas they have on learner independence. They set up a small action research project. They present their findings at the next IATEFL Conference.

The TD movement is in many ways parallel to the Learner Independence movement. Just as learners appear to make better progress when they make their own learning decisions, the chances are that teachers too will achieve better personal and professional growth when they take on personal responsibility for their own development.

(adapted from *Practical English Teaching*)

2 The article contains eight examples of teacher development. Put a tick next to those you would be interested in. Then compare your answers with a partner.

3 The words and expressions below are all from the article. *Without* reading the article again, decide whether they relate to TD or TT. Write TD or TT next to each one.

a) bottom-up
b) fixed agenda
c) inner-directed
d) continuing
e) peer-oriented
f) time-bound
g) hierarchical
h) top-down
i) problem solving
j) skills transmission

Practise saying the words and expressions and then compare your answers with a partner. Read the article again to check your answers.

4 Complete the chart below with words from the article, or words based on them.

Noun	Verb	Adjective(s)	Derived adjective(s)
development	develop		
	train		
			dissatisfied unsatisfactory
	educate		
	inform		
support			
		decided decisive	
qualification			
		dependent	

5 Now write sentences about yourself or a colleague with at least one of the words in each horizontal row. For example for *develop*:

I would like to develop my classroom management skills.

Then discuss your sentences with your partner.

6 Talking points

Talk about one or both of the points below with a partner or partners.

- Is teacher development more useful than teacher training?

- What opportunities for teacher training or teaching development are open to you?

3 Grammar: Indirect commands

1 Imagine some colleagues of yours have asked you for some advice about their work. Read the responses that you might give them in the bubbles below.

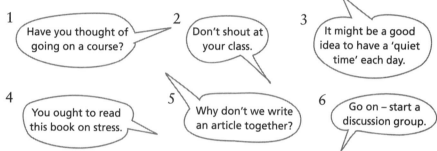

1 Have you thought of going on a course?

2 Don't shout at your class.

3 It might be a good idea to have a 'quiet time' each day.

4 You ought to read this book on stress.

5 Why don't we write an article together?

6 Go on – start a discussion group.

Now match the verbs below with the bubbles. You can match more than one bubble with each verb.

a) tell   d) suggest   g) invite
b) advise   e) encourage   h) warn
c) ask   f) recommend

2 Now write sentences with each of the verbs listed in Activity 1. For example:

I told her not to shout.

3 Which of the verbs in Activity 1 can be used with more than one structure?

4 Look at the picture. What would you advise this teacher to do? Write a line of advice for him.

Pool and discuss your ideas using the correct verb. For example, 'I would advise him to go on holiday' or 'I would recommend him to see his headteacher/director'.

I'M TIRED OF TEACHING

4   Student language: Assessing written work

1 The letter below was written in reply to a teacher trainer's offer to run a training session for a group of teachers in a school. The mistakes are under-lined.

Read the letter and then the list of skills below. Which skills do you think the writer is particularly good at?

Dear Miss Anne Newton,

Thank you very much for your ⓐ kindness to run a teacher-training session for our teachers. We appreciate that. ⓑ We ⓒ decide that the topic "Using pair and group work with large classes" would be helpful and serve our ⓓ need because there are a lot of students in our classes. ⓔ In addition, it is a good chance for us to brush our English.

We would like you to come on Friday 20th this ⓕ month, from 1.00 to 3.30 pm. The best way to get to Krabi from ⓖ Bangkok is to travel by coach and when you arrive the Krabi Bus Terminal around 7.00 am – 9.30 a.m., we will pick you up.

If any ⓗ inconvenience, please let me know by telephone 075-611181. I am looking forward to hearing from you.

Sincerely Yours

[signature]

(MR. PAISAN BOONPRAROB)

a) using appropriate vocabulary and expressions
b) sentence linking
c) paragraphing
d) using the appropriate register
e) using a suitable layout
f) using structures accurately

2 Which of the skills listed above contributes most to communicating the message of this letter?

3 Correct the underlined mistakes.

5   Writing: A letter

Imagine you have received the following letter. Read it, and then reply to it.

British Institute,
Marsanga

Dear Colleagues,
Following on from our very successful and enjoyable teacher-training course of last summer, I am writing to ask you if you would like me to come to your school to run a day-long seminar on one of the following:

— teaching large classes   — selecting coursebooks
— using group and pair work   — teaching pronunciation.

If you would like me to come, could you let me know which of these topics you would prefer and why, and also propose a date for the seminar? Could you also give me directions for how to get to your school?

I hope to hear from you soon and that we will be able to continue our work together.
My best wishes,

Clare Hanson
Clare Hanson

6   Speaking

1   Imagine you are attending a conference for teachers of English. Read the conference programme below and decide which sessions you would like to attend. Write them onto your conference planner on the next page.

Wednesday 3rd April			Room
1100–1155	MILLS	Inhibiting factors in language learning and use: the importance of anxiety	1
1100–1155	MATHEIDESZ	Games – do it yourself!	2
1100–1155	REMONDI	Teacher talk in the adult classroom	3
1100–1155	GAIRNS	Group feedback in teacher practice	4
1100–1155	VAUGHAN-REES	Rhymes and rhythm	5
1100–1155	BEALL	Poems as puzzles	6
1205–1255	PEARSON	Feedback: a trainee-centred approach on the RSA CERT TEFL course	1
1305–1355	SOSZYNSKA	Phrasal verbs without tears	1
1405–1455	HAWKINS	After advanced General English? – some ideas for classroom use	1
1530–1730	USHIMAR	BEST: Brainstorming, Editing, Summarizing and Transcribing	1
1530–1730	HITCHCOCK	Challenging the advanced learner: a programme rather than a course	2
1530–1730	HARGREAVES	Authentic business video: some approaches	3
1530–1730	STEVENS	Approaches to peer observation and teaching practice – feedback on teacher training courses	4
1530–1730	MORROW	Authentic writing tasks	5
1530–1730	REA-DICKENS	Approaches to classroom evaluation	6
1530–1730	CLEAVE	Doing it!	7

Conference Planner		
Time	*Talk*	*Room Number*
11.00–11.55		
12.05–12.55		
13.05–13.55		
14.05–14.55		
15.30–17.30		

2 Language functions

You want your colleague to attend the same session as you. To persuade him/her you may need to make suggestions or express preferences. Read the sentences below and decide if they are: (1) asking for information, (2) making suggestions, or (3) expressing preferences? Mark them 1, 2 or 3.

a) Why don't we go to this talk?
b) I'd rather go to the one in Room 3.
c) What about the talk in Room 4?
d) What time is it on?
e) Have you ever heard of this speaker?
f) Which talk would you like to go to?
g) I think the other talk might be more interesting.
h) Shall we go for a snack?
i) I'd quite like to hear the other talk.
j) I'd much rather not.

3 List the structures used above to (a) make suggestions, and (b) express preferences.

What other ways are there of expressing these functions?

4 Try to persuade a partner to attend the same session as you. Give reasons why it would be a good idea for them to attend the sessions you have chosen. Use as many expressions from Activity 2 as you find appropriate.

7   Listening

1 You are going to listen to an excerpt from a conference talk about teacher development. The words and expressions below occur in the talk. What do they mean?

a) to get into a rut
b) automatic
c) mechanical
d) formulaic
e) ritual (adj)
f) to lose touch with something
g) to refresh
h) tacit knowledge

2 Listen and decide:

a) Does the talk make teacher development seem relevant to your needs?
   How? Why?
b) Why are the words listed above central to this talk?

3 Listen again and decide if the following statements are True (T) or
False (F). According to the speaker:

a) After you've been teaching for a while you develop fixed routines for
   doing things.
b) You need to do some things automatically.
c) Automatic teaching leads to bored students.
d) TD helps you organise information-gap activities.
e) TD helps you understand why you do what you do.
f) TD helps you realise what you're good at.
g) Teachers must talk about their skills.
h) TD allows you to share knowledge with colleagues.

4 Talking points

• List some teaching activities which you do automatically.

• Tick those activities on your list that you might need to refresh.

• List some teaching activities that you think you handle well.

Discuss your answers with a partner or partners.

8   Classroom instructions: Introducing a true/false activity

1 A teacher might introduce Section 7, Activity 3 on page 61 with the instructions below. Read them, and then fill in the blanks.

> 'So, now you're going to listen to the excerpt again but this time for another reason. You'll need to listen much more carefully this time because you'll be listening (a) .... detail. When you listen I want you to decide (b) .... some statements are true or false. The statements are (c) .... Section 7, Activity 3 on page 61. Can you find them, please? (d) .... them?
>
> 'All right, now before you listen I'd just like you to read the statements through. If there's anything you don't understand (e) .... ask me. Was there (f) .... you didn't understand? Everything clear? OK, then I'm going to (g) .... you the cassette. As you listen, decide if each statement is true or (h) .... Put a T (i) .... the true ones and an (j) .... against the false (k) .... OK?'

2 Now introduce the same activity to a partner as if you were speaking to a class. Use your own words or those above.

9   Conclusions

1   Teaching-related vocabulary

In one minute, write down all the words and expressions you can think of related to teacher development. Then compare your answers with a partner's and/or with the vocabulary in this unit.

2   Reflections on teaching

- Has this unit helped you identify any areas of teacher development which you would like to follow up? What are they?

- What might be some ways of doing so?

8 Student development

1 Starter activities

1 Look at the photographs below. Do these students need or want the same thing from school or college? Can schools or colleges give all these students what they need and want?

Discuss your answers with a partner.

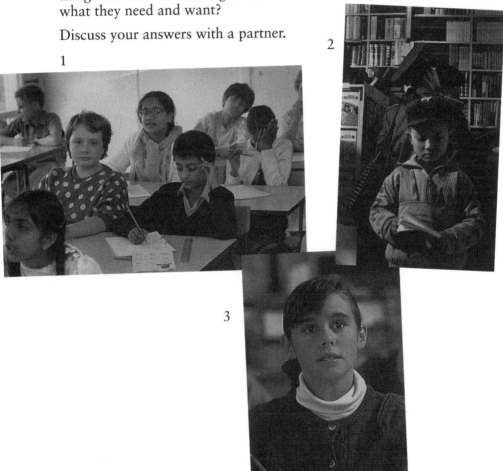

1

2

3

2 Reading

1 The four passages on the following two pages were written by school-leavers in Britain as part of a survey on 'My Perfect School'. Read the passages and note down in a few words in the bubble beside each face the main things each school-leaver would want from a perfect school. N.B. The passages contain some language mistakes.

a) My perfect school would be much like the one I went to. However several improvements could be made. There could be a better pupil–teacher relationship, especially between older teachers and pupils. Pupils should once again be given some kind of incentive to do well both at academic and sports activities. Dicipline would be strict but punishment would only be administered in severe cases. Any punishment administered would have some relevence to the crime commited instead of corporal punishment and lines. Pupils would also be given more career information to prepare them more fully for going out into the world. They would also be told that unemployment is a fact of life that they may have to live with. School would still be compulsory.

b) My pefect school would be a new modern school which is brightly decorated. I would like the school to let you do any subject that would get you the right qualification to get you the job that you were seeking and be able to sit any number of o grades. The teacher should be able to talk to us like a person and not a child and we should be able to talk freely with the teachers about your school work and any problems that you have. I do think that you should go to school because you would never get any where with out being educated. The rules in the school should be fair not to strict and not to lenient.

   This school would be fantastic compared to the school that I went to. The school was so cold and dreary and you could not talk freely to the teachers about your school work, and I did not like the way they just past you by because you were not the brightist kid in school.

c) My school would start at 10.00 am too 6.00 pm because 8.00 am is too early. The school would be a new school and have heated classrooms and decent PE equipment. The teachers would understand your problems and listen to your ideas. I would do a way with RE and music and bring in something about life after school. Jobs marriage sex etc. You would'nt have to wear school uniforms and you should be able to wear what you want. You have to do aleast three years of schooling at secondry. There would be longer break times. My school would be much better than the school I went too. My old school was to old fashioned you could'nt even come in with dyed hair or a short hair cut.

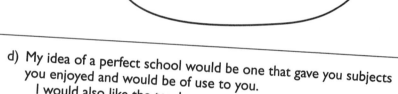

d) My idea of a perfect school would be one that gave you subjects you enjoyed and would be of use to you.
I would also like the teachers to treat us with more respect and intelligence instead of looking upon us as an inferior race. how are we supposed to treat them with respect when it is not returned and appreciated. I would like to go to a school that the teachers made an effort to communicate with you.
I think they shouldn't give you subjects like history, geography, science etc they may be quite intresting to some people, I liked history at school, but they are not practical and do not prepare you for life outside school; I think you should be prepared for looking for jobs what to expect etc from 1st yr at school in this day and age with the mess our country is in it is about the most sensible thing to do.

(from *The Best Years*: ed. J. M. Hughes)

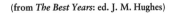

O→   **2** Is there any one thing that all these school-leavers wanted from school?

O→   **3** The words below are from the passages. Match those in the left-hand column with the appropriate one(s) in the right-hand column, as in the example.

a) strict ——— uniform
b) to give   subject
c) career   (a) punishment
d) academic ——— discipline
e) lenient   incentives
f) corporal   lines
g) school   relationship
h) decent   information
i) pupil–teacher   P.E. equipment

Now read through your answers and tick those that are common in your country. Discuss your answers with a partner.

4 Talking points

Talk about one or two of the points below with a partner or partners.

• The school-leavers above had strong opinions on school discipline, school buildings, subject choice, etc. In secondary schools, how much should the students be consulted on how to run the school?

• What did you enjoy most about your own experience of school?

• What helped you develop as a student?

3   Grammar: The second conditional

O→   **1** The sentences below are from the reading passages in Section 2. Read them and say whether they are talking about something that has been, something that might be, or something that hasn't been.

a) Discipline would be strict . . .
b) Pupils would . . . be given more information . . .
c) My perfect school would be a new modern school which is brightly decorated.
d) My school would start at 10.00 a.m. . . . .

2 What would your perfect school be like, for you as a teacher? Write three sentences, starting 'It would . . . '. Discuss your answers with a partner.

3 Now complete the sentences with the verbs in brackets.

    a) If we .... (have) more money we could paint the school.
    b) If there .... (be) more teachers in the school we could give students more career information.
    c) If teachers .... (not teach) so many hours they could have more time to talk to their students.
    d) If students always .... (choose) all their own subjects to study they would have to think hard about their futures.

4 Complete the rule on how to form the second conditional tense.

If + the .... tense + ... + infinitive without *to*

5 Write three sentences about your students' development, using *if* and the second conditional. For example:

If my students were more motivated they would study harder.

Then compare and discuss your answers with a partner.

4   Student language: Assessing written work

The letter below is from a student at an EFL summer school in Britain. It is in reply to a request from the school principal for the students' opinions of the school's services and the accommodation it provides.

Read the letter and:

a) Decide if the student is satisfied or not with the school.
b) Find the mistakes in the letter. Then correct them.
c) List the mistakes you would point out to the student.

Dear Joan,
    Thank you for you letter when I recived from my teacher, I would to tell you my opinion about my school, The services it is good, but the social activitie not to bad because the price for the trip it's quit high I hope to be cheap, about the accommodution its good only the shower it's bad because the water it's hot. there Isn't cold water and the Kitchen there no Kettel for a tea and Suger and mag to drink tea.
    That's is only my problem with the school.
        Thank you again   faisal

5   Writing: A letter

Imagine you are a student at the school you teach in now. Write a letter to a friend saying what you think of the school and how you would like it to change.

Then display and discuss your letters.

6   Speaking

1 Complete the sentences with your opinions about your current school.

a) School rules should allow students to . . .
b) The school syllabus should allow students to . . .
c) Student–teacher relationships should allow students to . . .
d) School facilities should allow students to . . .

2 Language functions

The expressions below are ways of asking for clarification. Read them and then discuss your sentences from Activity 1 with a partner. Use any of the expressions that you find useful.

What do you mean by . . . ?
What does . . . mean?
Sorry, what did you say?
Sorry, I didn't quite understand.
How do you say . . . ?

What's the English for . . . ?
What do you call it when you . . . ?
Could you speak a little more slowly /
   a bit louder?

7   Listening

1 One thing that most students want from school, of whatever kind, is a good teacher. Read the descriptions below of some children's favourite teachers. Are any of them similar to your own favourite teacher at primary school?

  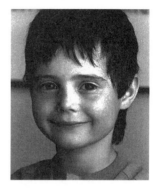

'My teachers are very kind and gentle. Mrs Johnson is my favourite one because she's got lovely black hair.'
Hannah, aged five

'I like all my teachers. Mrs Mortimer is my favourite because she wears glasses and she teaches us funny songs.'
Sarah, aged six

'My favourite teacher is Miss Renals. She's quite good, she doesn't usually get cross with me, but she does get cross with Hollie sometimes.'
Thomas, aged five

'I think teachers are quite good. Binny the helper is my best one because she's very good at doing the reading.'
Louise, aged four

'My teachers are good. Miss Simms is my favourite because she's my form teacher and she's very kind.'
Simon, aged eight

(from *Options*)

2 List the characteristics of a good teacher. Discuss your answers with a partner.

3 You are going to listen to Emmah, an eighteen-year-old British student, talking about what she thinks are the qualities of a good teacher.

Listen and tick those factors on your list from Activity 2 that Emmah mentions.

4 Listen again and list any other characteristics Emmah mentions.

5 What is the main message that Emmah would give teachers? Choose from this list.

Be patient.   Enjoy teaching.
Empathise with your students.   Help your students.
Be sociable.   Be tolerant.

Do you agree? Why/Why not?

8 Classroom instructions: Introducing a grammar activity

1 A teacher might introduce Section 3, Activity 1 on page 66 with the instructions below. Read them, and then fill in the blanks.

'OK, now we're going to (*a*) .... some grammar work. Now, I've written four sentences (*b*) .... the board – they're all taken (*c*) .... the passages we've just read, so they're all about 'My Perfect School'. Now, (*d*) .... anybody tell me what these sentences have (*e*) .... common? Yes, that's (*f*) .... – they all contain *would*, they're all hypothetical, they're all (*g*) .... of the second conditional tense. And that's the grammar I'd like you to study now. OK, now, first (*h*) .... all, tell me – are these sentences talking (*i*) .... something that has happened, something that might happen, or something that hasn't happened?'

2 Now introduce the same activity to a partner as if you were speaking to a class. Use your own words or those above. Continue the instructions.

3 What kinds of students would this kind of approach to grammar be suitable for?

9   Conclusions

1 Teaching-related vocabulary

Read the list of nouns below which are based on vocabulary in this unit. They are qualities that students of all ages might look for in a teacher. Which ones have you experienced as a student? Which ones can you offer as a teacher? Which ones, if any, do you find difficult to give?

strictness	empathy
willingness to communicate	respect
gentleness	kindness
fairness	patience
understanding	tolerance

Discuss your answers with a partner.

2 Reflections on teaching

Write six rules for teachers who want to encourage student development. Then compare your answers with a partner and make them into a chart of rules. Display the chart on a wall.

9   Personal development

1   Starter activities

1 Think about your future for a few minutes. Then put a tick next to the face below which best corresponds to how you feel about it. Or draw another face which expresses more accurately how you feel.

2 Now use the pictures below to indicate how you feel about these particular times in your future: (a) 10 years from now, and (b) 30 years from now. Then compare and discuss your answers with a partner.

sun   fog   rain   snow   wind

2   Listening

1 You are going to listen to an interview with a British woman called Glo Singer. Listen and decide which one of the following topics she is talking about:

the importance of change in life   career choices
being with other people   looking forward to the future
growing old   keeping young

2 The words and expressions below are all used by Glo in the interview. Explain their meaning in this context to a partner as you would to a class of advanced students. Refer to the transcript of the interview on page 130.

a) self-esteem (line 5)   d) to take off (line 28)
b) how people tick (line 16)   e) stuck (line 51)
c) to go downhill (line 27)   f) energising (line 52)

3 Look at the adjectives below and then listen again. Underline the adjectives which you think best describe Glo and note down your reasons. Then compare and discuss your answers with a partner.

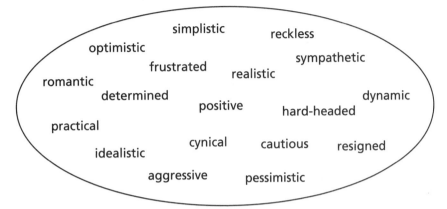

simplistic   reckless
optimistic   sympathetic
frustrated   realistic
romantic   dynamic
determined   positive   hard-headed
practical
idealistic   cynical   cautious   resigned
aggressive   pessimistic

4 Talking points

Read the statements below from the conversation with Glo. What is your opinion of them? Mark them with A (agree), D (disagree) or ID (it depends).

a) Life begins at 40.
b) Change is energising.
c) I don't want to know what I'll be doing in ten years' time.

Then compare and discuss your answers with a partner.

5 Look again at the adjectives in Activity 3. Do any of them describe people you know? If so, tick them.

Which characteristics are most important for personal development? Underline them.

Then compare and discuss your answers with a partner.

6 Mark the main stress on each adjective, consulting a dictionary and/or a colleague if necessary. Then say the words aloud.

3   Reading

1   The two poems below are by young people. Read them and then choose the most appropriate adjectives from those in Section 2, Activity 3, or your own, to describe their attitudes to old age.

Memories of a vegetable

Eighty-three years ago, he lay
In a white cradle, rocking, slowly.
Seventy-six years ago he blew out
Seven candles on a blue and white cake
With a little tin soldier
Standing to attention on top.
Sixty-nine years ago he turned fourteen,
His father died in the war.
His mother left home
In search of her lost love.
She too, was killed.
Sixty-two years ago he married.
Ten years later he divorced.
Another decade and he was middle-aged.
Thirty years ago, he met a
twenty-eight year old lady.
He asked her home and she slapped him
And walked out of his life.
Twenty years ago he went deaf,
Ten years ago he went blind.
Five years ago he was knocked down
By a car and paralysed.
He was put in a hospital
for the elderly and there he stayed.
Now he lies in a white bed.
Eighty-three years old.
A 'vegetable'.
But a vegetable with memories.

Claire Pearson, aged fifteen

An old woman

She sits alone
in a small dark room,
playing back the faded reel
of her memory,
and watching long-dead friends
playing tennis
on the screen in her mind.

She spends the summer sun
rocking by her window,
listening to youthful voices
laughing outside her solitude.
A newspaper lies unread on her lap,
her eyes have long given up
trying to drill the unruly words
into orderly lines.

With tidy stitches
she knits her loneliness
into long scarves
for reluctant grandchildren.
There is no bitterness in her heart
when they do not arrive,
only a cloud of resignation
that smothers her spirit.

Shaheen Ashraf, aged sixteen

(from *Cadbury's Fifth Book of Poetry*)

2   What seems to be the main way in which old people pass their time, according to these poems?

3   Read these poems to yourself, silently or aloud, to get into their mood.

4 Talking points

Talk about one or two of the points below with a partner or partners.

- How do you view old age?

- How do you see yourself in old age?

- Would young people in your country see old age in the same way as the writers of the poems in Activity 1?

4 Student language: Assessing oral communication

1 You are going to listen to two students: Maria from Spain and Takako from Japan. They are talking about how they see themselves in twenty years' time. Listen and decide which adjective in the circle on page 73 best describes their attitudes to their futures.

2 Listen again and make notes in the chart below about the students' attitudes to the topics listed there.

	Takako	Maria
Marriage	Wants to get married early	
Children		
Work/Staying at home		
Social life		

3 Takako and Maria manage to hold a good conversation with one another even though they use language inaccurately. How do they manage to communicate so fully with one another? Listen again and discuss your answers.

Can we draw any conclusions for the classroom from their achievements?

5 Grammar: Personal plans/intentions, personal predictions and certainties

1 Read the sentences below. Each expresses someone's view of their personal future. Which sentence expresses which view? Write *plan*, *intention*, *prediction* or *certainty* next to each one.

a) I think I'll probably find it hard to get a job.
b) I suppose I'll spend a lot of time commuting.
c) I'm visiting my friend this evening.
d) I'm going to get married when I'm about 25.
e) I'm buying a house in the country next month.
f) I'm going to stay at home and look after my children.
g) I imagine I'll have to move to another city.
h) I'm not going to work unless I absolutely have to.
i) I'll go to work every day.
j) I'll probably live in the country.
k) I'm giving up work next week.

Then compare and discuss your answers with a partner.

2 Which tenses were used in the sentences above to express:

a) personal plans/intentions?
b) personal predictions?
c) certainties?

3 What is your view of your future? Write down three certainties, three predictions and three intentions/plans about your future. Then discuss your views with a partner.

6 Speaking

1 Read the information below.

A ROLE PLAY: TO EMIGRATE OR NOT TO EMIGRATE?

Background information
You and your family (two parents and two children aged 20 and 24) are considering leaving your country for good and emigrating to Canada. There are various reasons why you are considering this: life in your country has become extremely expensive, inflation is very high, and neither the short-term nor the longer-term economic prospects are good. The present economic situation has affected everything negatively: job prospects, the quality of health care, personal security, the transport system, etc., etc. The whole family is worried about their futures.

Canada, on the other hand, has a solid economy, good job prospects and some of your relatives and friends already live there.

Nevertheless, the decision on whether to emigrate is not a simple one. It involves a big change and you do not all share the same point of view.

Mother
You want to emigrate. You think it will guarantee your children's future. You believe that you will be able to find a job as a university lecturer in maths and that your husband, as a doctor, will easily find a job. Though you will miss your own country and friends, you are confident you will soon make new friends and settle well and quickly into Canada. You have already been there twice and you really liked it. Generally speaking, you are a confident and optimistic person.

Father
You recognise that things are not going well in your country. Nevertheless, you are very attached to it. You love the way you spend your life there and you also have your elderly parents to consider. They would not emigrate and could you leave them? You think that as a doctor specialising in kidney diseases, you will always be able to make some kind of a living in your country, and hope that your children will probably fall on their feet. However, Canada may be a safer bet. You tend to be a rather conservative person.

Daughter
You are aged 20. You are doing a degree in engineering and you know that it is fairly unlikely that you will be able to find a job when you graduate. You already have job contacts in Canada and very good friends there. You also love the thought of being able to ski and do all the sports the Canadians do. However, you are concerned that your parents, especially your father, won't adapt well to the change. You are a very practical person.

Son
You are aged 24. You graduated in psychology last year. Since then you have been unemployed. You're currently going out with a girl you're thinking of marrying. She has a job – a good one – as a biologist. You've been to Canada and liked it a lot. You recognise that it would be sensible to emigrate there, but you have no wish to leave your own country. You want to work for its improvement and you feel you only belong there. You wouldn't like your parents to go without you. You are a little romantic.

Now divide into groups of four. Each person should take a role and prepare arguments and language in support of his/her position. Think also about what tenses you might want to use to talk about the future for plans, certainties or predictions.

2 Hold the role play as if it were a family discussion over lunch.

3 Now tell the rest of your colleagues what your 'family' has decided to do.

4 **Talking points**

Talk about one or both of the points below with a partner or partners.

- Would you ever contemplate making such a big change to your life as emigrating? Who would be affected by it?

- Have you made any big changes in your life? When? Why? How long did it take you to decide to make them? Do you want to make any big changes now?

7 **Writing: A letter**

Read the beginning of the letter below. It is from someone in the role play in Section 6 to a friend in Canada. Read the letter and complete it, as if you were the person you played in the role play. Tell your friend of the decisions you have made, how you (all) feel about them and what will happen next.

Then compare your letter with others in your group and display it.

> Dear Alex,
> I just thought I'd write to let you know what we've decided about coming to Canada. We all had a big talk about it at lunch time yesterday and

8   Classroom instructions: Setting up a role play

1 A teacher might set up the role play in Section 6 on pages 76-8 with the instructions below. Read them and then fill in the blanks.

> '(*a*) .... , everybody, today we're going to (*b*) .... a role play. It's (*c*) .... a family who're trying to decide (*d*) .... they should emigrate or not. Would you like to emigrate? . . . What do you think you would think about when trying to decide? . . . OK. Now I'm going to (*e*) .... you into groups (*f*) .... four and each group will be a family of four: mother, father and two grown-up children.
>
> 'But before I divide you (*g*) .... I'd just like you to read the information about the family which (*h*) .... on the sheets I'm going to give you.'

2 Now set up the same role play by talking to a partner as if you were speaking to a class. Use your own words or those above. Then continue the instructions.

9   Conclusions

1   Teaching-related vocabulary

Read the list below of words based on words in this unit. Which of them are most important for personal development? Number them in order of importance (1 = most important, 9 = least important).

security	energy
opportunities	qualifications
job prospects	friends
self-esteem	adaptability
confidence	

Then discuss your answers with a partner.

2   Reflections on teaching

- Did you find the role play useful and/or enjoyable? Why/Why not?
- Would/Could you do this role play with your own class? Why/Why not?

10 Job satisfaction

1 Starter activities

1 Look at the jobs above. Which three could you imagine yourself doing? Why might you find them satisfying? Discuss your answers with a partner.

2 Look at the list below of factors contributing to a teacher's job satisfaction. Number them in order of importance to you (1 = most important). Then compare and discuss your answers with a partner.

security of tenure   long holidays
good school equipment and resources   well-motivated students
a good salary   a pleasant school building
a good pension   a supportive headteacher
a sense of achievement   other (specify)

3 How satisfying do you find your present teaching job? Why?

2   Reading

1   The article below describes the lives of two Russian teachers of English, Anya and Olga. Read the article and find out whether they are satisfied with their jobs. Then compare and discuss your answer with a partner, giving reasons.

A tale of two teachers

At a time of unprecedented East–West interchange, Russia is losing its English teachers. Pieta Monks reports from Moscow.

'I would never work as a teacher after I qualify – never!' Anya's whole face expressed repugnance at the idea of being permanently stuck in a classroom with a lot of rowdy pupils. 'They don't even listen to me . . . '

She is a young, striking-looking, slim woman in her final year at the Moscow Pedagogical Institute – now upgraded to a university. She is very hard-working and able. She is at the moment on teaching practice, which she is finding difficult, hard and non-rewarding, financially and intellectually.

She looks even younger than her 21 years and lots of the children she teaches are bigger than her, and won't do what she tells them. There is also a dearth of good textbooks in her subject which is English.

She needs a powerful incentive to keep at it, which she won't get. Russian schools are crying out for English teachers, any English teachers, let alone those of the calibre of Anya.

English speakers can earn a fortune in private enterprise. On teaching practice Anya gets 3,000 roubles a month – a bit more than the basic rate for a teacher because she is at a special English school. Potatoes cost 80 roubles a kilo. A pair of shoes 3,000 roubles. She gets by because she lives at home. Her mother and father both work.

Of course, money isn't everything to Anya, but she naturally wants enough to live on, especially if she doesn't find the job that congenial anyway.

In the holidays she enjoyed working as an interpreter which paid three times her present pay.

Anya's rejection of the teaching profession is typical of her peers in college. Many of them, in fact, didn't even bother to finish the course but left once they found themselves profitable jobs in business, often earning, unqualified, more than their parents.

Olga Vinogradova is a lively, brilliant teacher, in her early thirties. She is an academic, who preferred to work in schools rather than carry on with her research. She teaches English, but did not train as a teacher. She is a graduate of the Institute of Linguistics, and worked on her thesis there, but found the professors stuffy.

She abandoned linguistics after getting her doctorate and became a computer expert, then an agricultural research scientist. Her English is excellent.

She was persuaded to go into teaching by the head of English at School No. 57, an inner city school. This was four years ago. She discovered that she enjoyed teaching and her pupils seemed to enjoy being taught by her.

She likes the new freedoms that allow her to teach the way she wants, as long as she broadly conforms to certain guidelines. A few years ago her timetable would have been rigidly controlled, even her 'voluntary' after-school work would have been strictly laid down.

There are particular problems in her inner city school. There are many Tartar children for whom Russian is not their first language, whose parents come to Moscow for work and whose living conditions are crowded and stressed. It is difficult to give special attention to them in classes of 40.

There are the general problems too which she shares with Anya: lack of textbooks and other teaching aids. For her, however, these are challenges that she can overcome.

But will she stay a teacher? Olga Vinogradova has two dependent children and a mother who suffers from Alzheimer's disease. She cannot afford to carry on working as a teacher if her salary does not improve.

Her husband earns twice as much as her, but in today's inflationary Russia they are finding it very difficult to simply get by. If a few years ago 20 per cent of their income went on food, today it is 80 per cent, leaving not enough for clothes and other basic necessities.

Anya and Olga are two women typical of today: Anya lured into private business that wouldn't have existed to tempt her a few years back, and Olga lured into teaching by the new freedoms and ideas that now abound there. Both women now can reject the careers they were trained for. But will Russian teachers get the salary they deserve and will Olga be lost to the teaching profession as well?

(adapted from *The Teacher*)

2 The words and expressions below are from the article. Read them and put a tick next to those whose meaning you know. Ask a partner or partners the meaning of the other words. Keep on asking until you can put a tick against each one.

a) rowdy (line 7)
b) teaching practice (line 11)
c) non-rewarding (line 12)
d) to keep at it (line 18)
e) calibre (line 21)
f) the basic rate (of pay) (line 24)
g) to get by (line 27)

h) unqualified (line 38)
i) to carry on with something (line 41)
j) to overcome (line 67)
k) to be able to afford (line 70)
l) to deserve (line 83)

3 Now put a dot (•) above the stressed syllables in each word or expression. Then check your answers with the cassette and repeat the words and expressions.

4 The sentences below describe Anya and Olga and their teaching situations. Read the sentences and decide which teacher each sentence is referring to. Put an A for Anya, an O for Olga, or A+O if it refers to both. Look back at the article if you need to.

a) She is hard-working.
b) She is on teaching practice.
c) Her pupils don't obey her.
d) There is a shortage of textbooks.
e) She is poorly paid.
f) She is a graduate.

g) She may not be able to afford to carry on teaching.
h) She has large classes.
i) She finds teaching stimulating.
j) She enjoys other work more.

5 Talking points

Talk about one or both of the points below with a partner or partners.

• Which of the statements in Activity 4 are true of you?

• Who do you have more sympathy with: Anya or Olga?

3 Grammar: Comparatives and superlatives

1 Read the sentences below and put a tick next to the grammatically correct ones. Then rewrite the others correctly.

a) Job security is so important as good pay.
b) Long holidays are usefuller than short working days.
c) Teaching is more rewarding than learning.
d) The most rewarding job is the one you like most.
e) A good pension is not so important as well-motivated students.
f) More rowdy pupils tend to learn better.

2 Are the rules below true (T) or false (F)? Correct those that are false.

a) The formation of comparative and superlative adjectives in English depends on the length of the adjective.

b) Adjectives of two syllables or less, or adjectives ending in *y*, add *er* to their stem to make the comparative, and *est* to their stem to make the superlative.

c) Adjectives ending in *y* change the *y* to *i* before adding *er* or *est*. No other spelling changes are required for the comparative or superlative of short adjectives.

d) To make the comparative of long adjectives you put *more* before the adjective, and to make the superlative you put *most* before the adjective.

3 Do you agree with the statements in Activity 1? Discuss them with a partner.

4   Speaking

1 These advertisements are all for jobs as English language teachers. Read them and see if you might be interested in applying for one of them. Talk about your choice with a partner.

SECONDARY TEACHERS OF ENGLISH, SCIENCE & MATHS

Time for a change and a new challenge?

Teaching in developing countries brings with it many challenges and rewards. New curricula and methods of operation, for example, give you the opportunity to become more resourceful and imaginative. And this is only part of the unique experience you will bring back with you to the U.K.

VSO has a number of urgent requests for Secondary Teachers in English, Maths and Science to fill jobs in **Kenya, Ghana, Uganda, Tanzania, the Caribbean, Zimbabwe, Malawi, Papua New Guinea, Belize, Guyana and the Pacific.**

Duties include classroom teaching and a variety of extra-curricular activities.

Positions are available for graduates as well as newly-trained and experienced teachers. VSO also welcomes applications from teachers who plan to take/have taken early retirement.

Relevant teaching experience is an advantage – but not essential.

For more details please complete and return the coupon below to: **Enquiries Unit, VSO, 317 Putney Bridge Road, London SW15 2PN.** Or telephone **081-780 1331** (24hr. ansaphone).

Conditions of work
- Pay based on local rates
- Equipment and re-equipment grants provided
- Rent-free accommodation usually provided ■ National insurance and medical insurance paid ■ Language training provided where necessary ■ Return flight paid ■ Posts (always approved by our field staff) are for a minimum of two years

VSO is working in
Anguilla Antigua/Barbuda Bangladesh Belize Bhutan

VSO

Volunteers working for a better world.

EFL TEACHERS urgently required full-time in Genoa, Italy. National contract terms. Candidates should be graduates with TEFL experience. Please express CV and recent photo to British srl, Via XX Settembre, 42 16121 - Genova, Italy.

EMIGRATE/WORK ABROAD: Australia, Canada, Europe, New Zealand & USA. Schools, Colleges, Addresses, Salaries. S.A.E. for details and prices to G. Harrison, 24 Church Street, Kirkby-in-Ashfield, Notts.

FRANCE Experienced Teachers - Business English - Car needed. Paris - Bordeaux - Montpellier - Lyon. Tel: 010 33 77 38 45

ITALY - ROME - TURIN - MILAN. Exciting opportunity! English Language Instructors needed who are energetic, dynamic and have strong clear voices. Pref. age 25–39. Tel: 010 396/970043

JAPAN English teachers required in Hiroshima, Japan. We are a well-established group of language schools with about 3,000 students of all ages. Our teachers are from Britain, America, Australia and New Zealand. The schools are both professional and very friendly. We mainly teach in our schools but we also supply teachers to secondary schools and universities in this area. The pay and working conditions are good.

We have positions in November, December and March.

Please send a C.V. and photo to: The Principal, D.E.H., 7-5 Nakamachi, Naka-Ku, Hiroshima, Japan, 730.

TURKEY Experienced Director of Studies required for language schools in Ankara. Also qualified teachers who have a university degree and RSA TEFLA. Tel 071 436 232 for an interview in London.

2 Language functions

You are thinking of applying for one of the jobs advertised on the previous page, but you are not sure. You talk to a friend to get some advice.

With a partner, take it in turns to be the possible applicant and his/her friend. If appropriate, use some of the expressions below for expressing uncertainty and for expressing enthusiasm.

I don't know if I'd like . . .	I'd really like to . . .
I don't know if I could cope with . . .	I'd love to . . .
I'm not sure if I'd manage . . .	I really fancy going . . .
I think I might (not) . . .	. . . sounds fantastic!

5   Listening

1 You are going to listen to a British teacher talking about a short working visit to a *gymnasium* (upper secondary school) in Denmark. Look at the list of features in the chart below and listen. Tick the features she mentions.

Pupil–staff ratio	
Teacher development programmes	
Class size	✓ *Set at 28, average 25*
School resources	
Holidays	
Contact time	
Clerical support	
Mixed-ability classes	
Cover for absent colleagues	
Paid maternity leave	
Form-filling	
Attendance in non-contact hours	
Staff meetings	
School buildings	
Paid lesson preparation time	

2 Listen again and note down the main points of each feature.

3 What can you learn about her teaching situation in Britain from her reactions to this *gymnasium*?

4 Talking points

Talk about one or both of the points below with a partner or partners.

- How does your teaching situation compare with the Danish one described in the interview?

- If there was one thing you could change to improve your job satisfaction, what would it be?

6   Student language: Assessing written work

1 Read the advertisement and the letter below. Which of the jobs in the advertisement is the letter writer interested in?

SUMMER VACANCIES
JULY–AUGUST

We have openings for people who love working with children.

SENIOR POSTS Develop your management skills this summer by running a top residential Summer Centre for overseas children aged up to 16.
EFL TEACHERS Qualified and experienced.
SPORTS COACHES Graduates/qualified coaches for various sports.

If you'd like more details, and an application form, write to:

The Director,
Summer Programmes,
Buckswood International
    Summer School,
Uckfield, East Sussex
Buckswood TN22 3PU

Dear sir,
    By the time I was thinking of my summer holiday I read your advertisement. I found that job of a teacher interesting as I am a teacher myself.
    I took my English language proficiency certificate 4 years ago and I've been teach English since then.
    I would appreciate if you sent me more details about this job especially in what concerns the payment and the accommodation.
    I thank you in anticipation.

    Fauzia Taleb.

2 Letters of inquiry about job vacancies are often organised as follows:

Paragraph 1: Introduction: saying where the writer read about the job
Paragraph 2: Summary of personal details such as age, nationality, qualifications, experience
Paragraph 3: Request for more information and an application form / Request for some other action

How far has the letter on page 85 followed this framework? Does it provide any unnecessary or inappropriate information?

3 Find and correct the language mistakes in the letter.

7 Writing a letter

1 Write your own letter inquiring about one or more of these jobs or those advertised on page 83. Follow the framework in Section 6, Activity 2 and ask for details that you need and for an application form.

8 Classroom instructions: Introducing pronunciation work

1 A teacher might introduce Section 2, Activity 3 on page 82 with the instructions below. Read them and then fill in the blanks.

'Now we're going to do some pronunciation work on word stress. Can you look at the words in Section 2, Activity 2 on page 82 and decide (a) .... the stressed syllable is in each word. The (b) .... syllable is the one that is (c) .... most emphasis when you're speaking, right? OK. Now what I'd like you to do is (d) .... the stressed syllable by putting a (e) .... above it. Then afterwards we're going to listen to the words (f) .... the cassette so that you can (g) .... your answers. Then after that I'll ask you to listen to the words on the cassette again and repeat them, and (h) .... you repeat them I'd like you to pay special attention to your word stress. OK, so, first mark the stress, then listen and check, and finally listen and repeat. Is (i) .... clear?'

2 Now introduce the same activity to a partner as if you were speaking to a class. Use your own words or the words above.

9   Conclusions

1 Teaching-related vocabulary

List at least four words from this unit under each of the headings below. Then add any others you can think of.

Reasons for job satisfaction   Reasons for lack of job satisfaction

Explain and discuss your answers with a partner.

2 Reflections on teaching

- Has your level of job satisfaction changed over the time you have been teaching? Why/Why not?

- Are there any ways in which you might be able to improve your colleagues' job satisfaction?

11 Organising your time

1 Starter activities

1 Look at the picture.

What does it suggest to you? What aspects of teaching do you find stressful? List them and discuss them with a partner.

2 Imagine that you have just got home from work one evening in the ninth week of the longest term. You have had a hard day and you're feeling tired. However, you haven't prepared your lessons for tomorrow. Read the list below of possible activities for this evening and decide which are the most urgent or important. Number them in order of priority (1 = high priority, 2 = medium priority, 3 = low priority).

- Visit/phone someone in your family (you haven't spoken to them for over a week).
- Think for a while about today's and tomorrow's problems at work.
- Do some shopping (there's no food in the house apart from supper).
- Clean the car (it's filthy).
- Prepare tomorrow's lessons.
- Do the washing (there aren't many clean clothes left).
- Cook the supper.
- Watch some television.
- Do some housework.
- Sit down and talk to your friends/family.
- Go to the cinema.
- Read a book on teaching methodology.
- Relax all evening.
- Go to bed early.
- Write an important and overdue letter to the bank manager.

Then discuss your priorities with a partner.

2   Reading

1   The article below describes a typical teaching day for Aneone Turner, a teacher in a British primary school. Read the article and decide how well she organises her time. Give her a score on the scale 1–5 (1 = well, 5 = badly).

A day in the life of a teacher

Aneone Turner, aged 38, has been teaching for 17 years. She currently teaches five- and six-year-olds in a Kent primary school which has 560 pupils. She has two school-age sons.

7.30 a.m. Aneone arrives at school: 'It's quiet and peaceful at that time and I can get some preparation done – photocopying worksheets for class.'

8.30 Playground duty as parents deliver their children: 'You usually end up with eight children hanging on to you. The parents may want a word – explaining how the dog chewed their child's exercise book last night, etc.'

8.45 Takes register for the 32 pupils in her class. Organises first and second lunch sittings.

9.00 School assembly.

9.15 'I start classes. Because I have so many pupils I have to split them into groups. And I really appreciate the help I get from parents. There is usually one mother helping out each morning. Typically I will start a maths group, then write some work on the board for an English group – they can get on with that on their own for a bit. My helper is taking the third group for a cookery lesson – they're making cheesy puffs this morning.'

10.30 Break: 'I have coffee in the staffroom with another teacher who helps me run the after-hours French club. We are working on a school exchange with a French school.'

10.45 Pupils back in class – finishing off the work they were set earlier.

11.15 'Showing time – well, that's what I call it. The pupils bring something to school that they have made or are interested in. They stand up and talk about it and I encourage the children to ask questions. I love this time.'

11.45 Reading: 'The whole school reads at this time. There are so many pupils I can't possibly hear them read even once a week. So I ask the parent helpers to hear them individually and I concentrate on those with difficulties.'

12 noon Lunch break. 'It's not my turn for lunch duty today.'

12.30 p.m. Staff meeting: 'We discuss safety measures in and around the school's two swimming-pools. We decide we need an expert to come and talk to us about it. Our Head isn't there – he is rushed off his feet organising a junior sports day. I go to test the pool temperature. It's cold.'

1.15 'If children don't want to swim (it's 65°F) I don't make them today. Most want to and I have to get three groups in and out in half an hour. It's a real hassle – all 32 of my pupils have to blow their noses, go to the loo, etc. before going in – and we have to put their swimming caps on.'

1.45 'At this time the children have to work out how to do a simple task. Today we have a big box with people in it and the challenge is to move it.'

2.15 Tea break: 'I dish out the swimming badges to those who have earned them.'

2.30 'The children who will be starting next term arrive with their mums to join us with some story reading. I want them to find friends.'

3.00 End of school day: 'I see that everyone goes home.'

3.30 Meeting with the three other teachers who teach the five- and six-year-olds. 'Because of the National Curriculum it is very important for us to make sure we are doing the same things. Two afternoons a week, I run the netball or French club. It's voluntary and I am afraid there is now so much other work that things like that will go.'

5.30 Go home; tea: 'See my children.'

6–7.00 'Preparation for following day. I am lucky that I have no marking to worry about. But I usually do an hour's work to prepare for the following day. There is also a lot more paperwork and bumf to read these days. I think teachers are overworked – but I try to feel positive about it despite the difficulties. My school has a terrific headmaster, which helps.'

(from *Options*)

2   Read the article again and complete the chart with the correct times.

	Time
Teaching	*9.15–10.30 a.m.*
Preparation	
Meetings	
Other duties (specify which):	

3 Some of Aneone's regular tasks are listed below. Read the list and tick the tasks that primary-school teachers in your country also do. Then underline those that you do.

do lesson preparation	attend staff meeting
photocopy worksheets	organise swimming classes
do playground duty	set a simple task
take the register	read stories aloud
attend school assembly	make sure that everyone leaves
split pupils into groups	run an after-school club
hear pupils read aloud	

Then tell a partner about the tasks that you do.

4 Talking points

Talk about one or two of the points below with a partner or partners.

- How does Aneone's timetable compare with yours?

- If you teach adults or older children, how are your activities different from Aneone's?

- Would you like to be a primary-school teacher in Britain?

3   Grammar: Questions

1 Read the mini-dialogues and complete them with appropriate questions. Then think of three more questions an interviewer might ask a teacher.

a) Interviewer: ....
    Teacher: Usually at nine fifteen – just after school assembly.
b) Interviewer: ....
    Teacher: Yes, I did some preparation last night after I'd eaten.
c) Interviewer: ....
    Teacher: We don't have enough teaching staff so we need parents to help.
d) Interviewer: ....
    Teacher: Usually in the evening, and then before lessons start in the morning.
e) Interviewer: ....
    Teacher: My father, really. He was a teacher himself and I'm sure he inspired me.
f) Interviewer: ....
    Teacher: I think so. I've no wish to do anything else.

2 Complete the rules on how to form questions in English.

 a) *Yes/No* questions
 .... + ... + infinitive without *to*
 b) *Wh*-questions
 Wh-word + ... + subject + infinitive without *to*
 c) These verbs do not use *do* to make questions: ....
 To make questions with these verbs you invert the .... and the verb.

4   Speaking

1 Read the questionnaire below and add any extra questions at numbers 12–13. Then complete the column *You*.

How good are you at organising your time at work?	You	Colleague

Punctuality
 1 Do you allow enough time to get to:
   a) work?
   b) your lesson?		

2 Do you keep your breaks to the right length?		
3 Do your lessons usually last the right length of time?		
Lesson time 4 When do you plan your lessons?		
5 When do you make any materials for your lessons?		
6 Do you always check beforehand that 'machinery' for your lesson is working?		
7 When do you get together your books, etc. for your next lesson?		
8 Do you find the correct place on a cassette/video before the lesson?		
9 How quickly do you usually return your students' homework?		
Social contacts 10 Do you allow too little/enough/too much time for exchanging ideas with colleagues?		
11 Do you allow too little/enough/too much time for talking with students?		
Other 12		
13		

2 Ask a partner questions to complete the *Colleague* column.

3 Talking points

Talk about one or both of the points below with a partner or partners.

Judging from your answers to the questionnaire:

* how well do you plan your teaching time?

* what could you do to improve?

5   Student language: Assessing oral communication

1 Listen to a conversation between two students and answer the questions.

   a) What are they talking about?
   b) What nationality(ies) do you think they are?
   c) What language level do you think they are?

2 Listen again, this time concentrating only on the main speaker. Note down ten grammar or vocabulary mistakes she makes.

Then compare your answers with a partner. Did you note down the same mistakes? Why/Why not?

3 Talking points

Listen again and decide:

* is the main speaker's English easy for you to understand?

* would you interrupt these students to correct them if they were doing this pair work in your class?

6   Writing: A letter

1 Imagine that Aneone (see Section 2) has just become your penfriend. Read the last part of the imaginary letter from her below. Then write a reply.

> *Please let me know what your teaching day is like. Is it very different to mine?*
> *Looking forward to hearing from you,*
>   *Yours*
>   *Aneone*

7   Listening

1 You are going to listen to a British primary-school teacher, Monica Battersby, talking about her job. She talks about the five topics which are listed in order below. Listen and fill in the blanks.

a) the .... of the children in her class
b) her ....aims
c) the different .... the children work in class
d) the different .... she does with the children
e) .... at home and school

2 Look at the five groups below of words and expressions based on the interview. Then listen again and match the groups with the topics (a)–(e) in Activity 1.

<table>
<tr><td>

1
reading
number work
science
art and craft
manipulative skills

</td><td>

4
organising groups
getting the apparatus ready
making paints and glue
working in the evening
   and at weekends

</td></tr>
<tr><td>

2
mixed class
Reception and Year 1

</td><td rowspan="2">

5
assembly
group activities
story times
P.E. times
music times

</td></tr>
<tr><td>

3
project work
group work
whole class work
individual work

</td></tr>
</table>

3 Put a dot (•) above the stressed syllables in the words and expressions in Activity 2. Then check your answers with the cassette and repeat the words and expressions.

4 Interview a partner using the list of topics in Activity 1 to structure your interview. Then change roles.

8   Classroom instructions: Introducing pair work

1 A teacher might introduce the pair work in Section 4, Activity 2 on page 92 with the instructions below. Read them and then fill in the blanks.

'Right, now, we're going to do (a) ………… pair work – just working (b) …………
twos, Maria and Pedro together, José and São, Isabel and João, etc., etc. OK,
now, I'm going to give (c) ………… this questionnaire. Look at it – it's got two (d)
………… . Fill in the first one about yourself, and then, with your partner, ask (e)
………… other the questions and write the answers (f) ………… the boxes in the
columns.

'OK, so do you understand what you've (g) ………… to do? Ana, could you
(h) ………… me? Yes, that's right. You ask one another the questions and then
you write the answers in the (i) ………… . (j) ………… the way, when you're
writing the answers, don't write great long answers, just notes, OK? Just the
most important thing your partner's said. All right, now (k) ………… you start
by just reading the questions?'

2 Now introduce the same activity to a partner as if you were speaking to a class. Use your own words or those above.

9   Conclusions

1   Teaching-related vocabulary

Look through this unit and find at least ten words related to a teacher's timetable that are relevant to you. Then discuss your list with a partner.

2   Reflections on teaching

The following activities were in this unit:

a prioritising activity (Section 1, Activity 2)
a questionnaire used as a basis for interaction (Section 4, Activity 2)
a matching activity (Section 7, Activity 2)

- Which of these activities requires the most careful organisation of time either in or out of class?

- In which of your school activities or lessons is organisation of time a critical factor? How do you deal with this?

12 A teacher's character

1 Starter activities

1 Look at the pictures. Which of the people would you have liked as your teacher? Why? Why not?

1

2

3

4

2 Read the list of character traits below. Which are the five most important traits for a teacher? Number them in order of importance (1 = most important, 5 = least important). Then compare and discuss your answers with a partner.

dynamism	generosity	patience
thoughtfulness	toughness	calmness
care for people	intelligence	flexibility
sense of humour	determination	sensitivity
love of performing	enthusiasm	imagination

3 Tell your partner about a teacher at school who made a big impression (positive or negative) on you. Describe their character.

2   Reading

1 Read the passage below about a primary-school teacher. Then answer the question: What was the secret of this teacher's magic?

Everything changed in the second year. There must have been just as many children in the classroom, but somehow the room seemed bigger than the one we had left. Perhaps it was because everything was in order in that classroom, everything was in its proper place. There were corners for this and corners for that, our desks had our names stuck on them, so we knew our place. So did Miss Craddock. You could never go into that room when she wasn't there. In the mornings she looked just the same as we had left her in the evenings. She was never absent or late for school. Sometimes I wondered if she might have slept there.

Miss Craddock was very tall, one of the tallest women I have ever seen. She wore flat shoes; I don't know what her clothes looked like because I never saw her with any on. That is, I never saw her in a frock, or a pullover and skirt. Two large smocks covered her up; they buttoned down the front. One of them was patterned with blue and white daisies, the other one was of pink-and-white check. I liked the daisies one best; I think she must have done too because she wore it more than the pink-and-white one. She never buttoned them, even the two buttons at the top, but she might have buttoned these up had her neck not been so long. She said herself that she looked like a giraffe, yes she did, when she was showing us pictures of animals. Miss Craddock didn't mind us laughing when she told us this, she laughed herself.

Giraffes are beautiful animals and that is why I fell in love with Miss Craddock. I think that is why, although her eyes were big and blue, her complexion fresh, she always smelled as though she had just got out of the bath, she smelt of clean washing, no scent to her just this clean smell.

How would you know what a teacher smelled like? Well, at some time during the day Miss Craddock would cuddle us. Hold us quite close to her and say something very special. We all got the same treatment. As I had never had it at home I suppose I appreciated it more than some of the others. The room was never noisy like the other one had been, this was funny because I can't ever remember Miss Craddock shouting. There were eight groups for reading lessons and she would float from group to group. I can't remember how she taught us to read, in fact I can't remember not being able to read. I had not been in her class long before she extracted me from the groups altogether; she would give me a book that she had brought from home or borrowed from her friend Miss Moore and tell me to read it on my own. Later, she would ask me what the book was about.

'Well now, Tommy, and what do I start you on next, we can't
have you standing still, can we?' I didn't know who the other
person was when she said 'we' because she hadn't married. I had
mentioned to my dad that I'd like to marry her.

'Ah, and you could do a lot worse,' was his reply. I never asked
her, I couldn't, although I would have liked her arms around me
much more than my daily ration.

Even playtimes were different in Miss Craddock's class. Other
teachers disappeared down the corridor into a small room, but
Miss Craddock always sat behind her desk. She would send one of
us for her morning hot milky drink. This was an honour and we all
sat up and looked at her appealingly, hoping that she would choose
us to do her a favour. Most of the class went out to play like the
rest of the school, but if you wanted to stay inside you could, and if
any child had a cold or Miss Craddock thought that they were not
well, she would have them in the room with her. I rarely went out
to play. I read, sometimes I just talked to her when there weren't
too many children in. She was interested in everything and I never
had met anyone who could listen as well as she could. Not that I
thought she was perfect. No, she told lies, I think they were lies
although she never went red when she told them, so for her
perhaps they weren't lies at all.

(from *Forties Child*: Tom Wakefield)

2 Which of the adjectives in the chart below best describe Miss Craddock?

Adjective	Noun
gentle	gentleness
cheerful	
affectionate	
sentimental	
dedicated	
reliable	
clean	
ordered	
lively	

3 Now complete the chart with the nouns of the adjectives. Then pronounce
the adjectives and their noun forms.

4 How would you describe Tommy's character?

5 Talking points

Talk about one or two of the points below with a partner or partners.

- Would you have liked Miss Craddock as your primary-school teacher?

- In your opinion, is it better for boys to have women teachers and girls to have men teachers?

- Do you think adult learners are affected by having teachers of the same/ different gender? Why/Why not?

- What adjectives best describe you as a teacher?

3   Grammar: The third conditional

1 Make sentences from the words provided, as in this example:

Tommy wouldn't have loved Miss Craddock so much if:
she/not/give him cuddles

She hadn't given him cuddles.

Tommy wouldn't have loved Miss Craddock so much if:

a) she/not/be sweet-smelling
b) she/pay him less attention
c) she/not/love teaching so much
d) she/behave less reliably
e) she/not/look like a giraffe

2 Now write five sentences about when you were at school/college/university. For example:

I wouldn't have gone to university if my teachers hadn't encouraged me.

Then compare and discuss your sentences with a partner.

3 When do you use the third conditional? Choose the right answer:

a) To talk about imaginary or hypothetical events or states.
b) To talk about past events or states that aren't true.
c) To talk about hypothetical past events or states.

4   Listening

1   In your opinion, what might be the character traits required by a teacher who wishes to go and work in a foreign country? Write a short list.

2   You are going to listen to a recruitment manager whose job is to recruit teachers for a wide range of jobs all over the world. Here he is talking about what he looks for in a candidate. Listen and find out which of the things in the list below he looks for during an interview.

behaviour   qualifications
experience   personality

3   Read the words and expressions below which the speaker uses. Put them into the most appropriate category of these three:

Behaviour   Qualifications   Personality

a diploma   a degree
outgoing   to fiddle with something
nervous   to grab a chair
eye contact   ability to reflect

4   Listen again and make brief notes in the chart below on what the speaker looks for before and during an interview. Then discuss your answers. Is he looking for any of the things you listed in Activity 1?

| Behaviour | Qualifications | | Personality |
	Inexperienced people	Experienced people	
	University degree		

5   **Talking points**

Talk about one or both of the points below with a partner or partners.

- If you were interviewing someone to work in your department or school would you be looking for the same characteristics as this recruitment manager? How would you recognise them?

- If you went for an interview yourself, how could you get across your qualities as a teacher?

5   Speaking

1   Read the advertisement and then, with a partner, list the qualities, experience and qualifications you would look for in someone applying for one of these jobs.

> **EUROPEAN LANGUAGE CAMPS**. The Schools Unit is looking for over 100 teachers and 6th formers to help at several Language camps in Turkey, Poland and Hungary for 3 weeks. Participants assist with teaching English and social activities, drama, music, sports and crafts. For application forms write to or phone Alan Bell, Central Bureau, Seymour Mews House, Seymour Mews, London W1H 9PE. Tel: 071-486 5101.

2   You are going to interview some candidates for these jobs. You have noted down the questions below which you want to ask them. Number them in the order you want to ask them (1 = first question).

Do you have any specialist areas?
How soon could you start?
When did you get your . . . certificate?
Do you prefer working with students of particular ages/levels?
Can you offer any extra skills like drama, music or sports?

3   Write six further questions you would ask an applicant for the above jobs.

4   With a partner, role play an interview for one of the jobs. The 'interviewer' should use the questions from Activities 2 and 3. The 'candidate' should give details of an imaginary (un)suitable person.

6   Student language: Assessing oral communication

1   You are going to listen to two students talking: Harako from Japan, and Carla from Spain. Listen and find out:

a) what they are talking about
b) whether Harako makes mistakes in any of the areas in the list below:

tenses	articles
question formation	word order
countable v uncountable nouns	singulars and plurals
pronunciation	sentence formation

2   Listen again and write down an example of each type of mistake. Which, if any, of these mistakes would you try to make Harako aware of? How? Compare and discuss your answers with a partner.

7 Writing: A reference

1 Imagine that a colleague of yours has applied for one of the jobs in Section 5 and that you have been asked to write a letter of reference for him/her. Write a character reference describing your colleague's personality, teaching experience, teaching abilities, etc.

8 Classroom instructions: Introducing a vocabulary activity

1 A teacher might introduce the vocabulary work in Section 1, Activity 2 on page 95 with the instructions below. Read them and then fill in the blanks.

'OK, now on page 95 you've got a list of fifteen nouns. Can you find them, please? Got them? OK. Now, all these nouns refer (a) .... character traits and (b) .... I'd like you to do is to read (c) .... the nouns and decide which (d) .... you think are the most important character traits for a teacher to have. I'd like you to number the nouns (e) .... you think are the five most important ones. Number them 1 to 5, and put the number one (f) .... the trait which you think is really the most important of all, then 2, 3, 4 and 5 against the others (g) .... descending order of importance. (h) ...., all you have to do is select the five most important traits and (i) .... them. Is that clear? OK.'

2 Now introduce the same activity to a partner as if you were speaking to a class. Use your own words or those above.

9 Conclusions

1 Teaching-related vocabulary

This unit has concentrated on adjectives that describe *teachers'* qualities. With a partner, list ten adjectives that, in your opinion, describe a 'good' *student's* qualities. Then compare and discuss your answers with others.

2 Reflections on teaching

Look through this unit and decide which activities you could/couldn't use with your own students. Consider the level of your students, their age, their motivation and the type of teaching and learning approach used in the activity.

13 Trouble in the classroom

1 Starter activities

1 Look at the pictures of some five- and six-year-old British children which were drawn by the children themselves. What kind of personalities do you think these children might have? Do you think any of them might be difficult to teach?

Discuss your answers with a partner.

2 What kinds of pupils/students do you find it difficult to teach? Why?

2 Reading

1 Read the passage below about a child with behavioural problems. Decide
how you would deal with Daniel if he was a pupil of yours. Discuss your
answers.

Nine-year-old Daniel was . . . troublesome at school. His parents
were well off, but they were divorced. Daniel was in the habit of
pushing children for no apparent reason, and on one occasion he
scratched a girl's leg with a cocktail stick until it bled. ...In spite of
this very objectionable behaviour, the teacher reported that there
was something very appealing about Daniel when she talked to him
and reprimanded him.

Daniel was also a problem at home. There was a close connection between his home circumstances and his behaviour at school.
He lived with his mother and a younger brother with whom Daniel
quarrelled all the time. Mother preferred the younger brother,
who was much better behaved at home and much more successful
at school than Daniel. The mother tried not to favour her younger
son, but she was aware of her preferences.

It seemed very obvious that Daniel's attacks on other children at
school were connected with his jealousy of his younger brother.
He attacked his brother at home, just as he attacked the children
at school. His attacks on his brother were, of course, linked to his
feelings of being unwanted and unloved at home. They also
ensured that his mother took notice of him. Similarly, his attacks
on the other children at school necessitated the teacher's attention. Once he had the teacher's attention, e.g. when she talked to
him, he could be very appealing. Just as his frequent quarrels with
his younger brother can be seen as his way of telling his mother
that he felt hurt by her preference of the younger child, he showed
his teacher how hurt he was by her attending to other children.
Neither the mother nor the teacher neglected him. Neither of
them could give him as much attention as he desired. The reasons
for Daniel's insatiable greed for attention were very complex and
complicated and not easy to discover.

Daniel's attention-seeking behaviour made the teacher's life very
difficult. She understood that he wanted attention and that he
needed it, yet as one of forty children he could not get what he
wanted. She also had to protect the other children from his
attacks. So she had to reprimand him and punish him, just as his
mother did at home. In this way Daniel was caught in a vicious circle which was difficult to break. He wanted to be loved, he felt
angry because he could not get what he wanted, he attacked other
children because he was angry, and therefore could not get the
love he wanted.

(from *Troublesome Children in the Classroom*: Irene Caspari)

2 The words and expressions below are taken from the passage about Daniel. They are used to describe (a) Daniel, (b) his brother and (c) his mother. Which word or expression is used to describe whom?

objectionable	troublesome
appealing	unloved
divorced	angry
better behaved	attention-seeking
hurt	caught in a vicious circle

Now pronounce each of the words and expressions.

3 Read the passage again and make brief notes on the following:

a) Daniel's classroom behaviour
b) Daniel's behaviour at home
c) the causes of Daniel's behaviour
d) how Daniel's teacher treated him.

Then compare your answers with a partner.

4 Talking points

Talk about one or both of the points below with a partner or partners.

- Do you think psychotherapy might have helped Daniel and his mother?

- Have you ever had a student – child, or adult – like Daniel? What did you do about them?

3   Grammar: The definite article

1 The passage below is an extract from a newspaper article about violence in a school in New York. Read it and then fill in the blanks with *the* where necessary.

Thomas Jefferson High School is a five-storey redbrick building occupying an entire block on Pennsylvania Avenue, in the East New York section of Brooklyn. All the windows on the lower three floors are protected by iron grilles and the main entrance doors are of steel.
   Shortly before 10.30 a.m. on (a) .... Monday, November 25, a fight broke out between (b) .... two students in a third-floor hallway. Fourteen-year-old Jason Bentley saw that his brother was one of those involved. Intending to help his brother, he pulled out of his knapsack (c) .... 9mm automatic pistol that he had bought on (d) .... street for $50. (e) .... boy his brother was fighting saw (f) .... gun and began retreating down (g) .... corridor. Jason, in a panic, fired three shots. Children in (h) .... crowded hallway scattered, screaming with (i) .... terror. (j) .... first slug hit (k) .... ceiling. (l) .... second hit Robert

Anderson, 48, a teacher, who had been coming to intervene; he staggered into a nearby classroom, wounded in (*m*) .... neck. (*n*) .... third bullet hit Darryl Sharpe, aged 16, who fell to (*o*) .... floor with (*p*) .... blood pumping from his neck and collecting in a pool on (*q*) .... polished stone floor. Darryl died in (*r*) .... hospital before noon. Jason Bentley fled (*s*) .... school, but was arrested later that day on homicide charges.

(from *Sunday Times Magazine*)

Then compare your answers with a partner.

2 Complete this rule for the use of *the*:

Generally speaking, in English, *the* is used to refer to:
• (*a*) .... things, e.g. *The box on the table*.
• things that have (*b*) .... been mentioned, e.g. *I saw a boy and a girl. I didn't really notice the boy, but the girl was very smartly dressed.*
• things that are considered (*c*) .... e.g. *the sun*.

It is *not* used:
• when referring to (*d*) .... things, e.g. *There was a box on the table.*
• when referring to classes of things in (*e*) .... e.g. *Children often need a lot of attention.*

4 Speaking

1 Read the descriptions of three students and decide how you would deal with each one. Then write a similar description of a student of yours who concerns you.

L. is seven. He is very bright, as his contributions to discussions and his oral work show. However, in his written work he has great problems concentrating. As a result, his reading and writing are poor. This is affecting his performance in all subjects and may be affecting his general motivation. He seems to be a sociable and friendly boy.

J. is sixteen. She has missed a lot of school lately through truanting. She seems unhappy and other pupils tease her a lot as she is very fat. Her father is unemployed and her mother has a drink problem. In her lessons, she is inattentive and shows little interest.

M. is a 36-year-old lawyer. He joined your evening class of adults last term. He always arrives late, is very noisy when he arrives and sits complaining and talking through most of the lessons. He disturbs the other students who have started complaining to you about him. Although he says he really needs to learn English for his work, he doesn't seem to be very interested and doesn't work very hard.

2 Language functions

Read the expressions below which are ways of introducing opinions in English. Add other ways to the list.

> I think . . .   In my experience . .
> As far as I'm concerned . . .   What I've found is that . . .
> From what I can see . . .

3 With a partner, talk about what you would do to help the three students described in Activity 1. Use as many of the ways of introducing opinions as you find appropriate.

5   Listening

1 Do you agree with this quotation from a British educational newspaper?

> There are teachers who lack confidence in their ability to deal with disruption and who see their classes as potentially hostile. They create a negative classroom atmosphere by frequent criticism and rare praise. . . . Their methods increase the danger of major confrontation not only with individual pupils but with the whole class.
>
> (from *The Times Educational Supplement*)

2 How do you think teachers can 'manage' their classrooms so as to avoid discipline problems and encourage better learning? Make a list of possible ways and then discuss your answers with a partner.

3 Listen to a teacher suggesting ways in which teachers can manage their classrooms better. Look at your list from Activity 2 and put a tick next to the ways the teacher mentions.

4 Look at the list below of some things teachers can do in the classroom. Listen again and tick those which, according to the teacher, improve classroom management.

a)   Make your classroom look attractive.
b)   Show videos.
c)   Arrange furniture in the way you need.
d)   Move around the room a lot.
e)   Decide where pupils should sit.
f)   Plan a range of work to suit everyone.
g)   Vary your activities.
h)   Repeat all instructions.
i)   Have quiet times and noisier times.
j)   Praise rather than punish.
k)   Be consistent in your behaviour.
l)   Never threaten.
m)   Run for help when you need to.
n)   Evaluate your lessons.

5 Talking points

- Do you agree with the advice given by the teacher in Activity 4? Discuss with a partner or partners.

- Read the list below of teacher responses to students' inappropriate behaviour. Number them in order (1 = most severe, 13 = least severe). Then compare your answers with a partner.

  - restraining touch
  - pausing
  - quiet private word (friendly or unfriendly)
  - pointing
  - specific prohibition (with or without sarcasm, smile, hostility or glee)
  - looking
  - class punishment
  - actual punishment, immediate or deferred (e.g. removal from room, detention, extra work, lines, letter home, sent to more senior staff)
  - specific prohibition with unnamed (mysterious) sanction
  - naming
  - naming, pointing and looking
  - public telling off / putting down
  - shouting

  (adapted from 'Classroom Discipline': Clifford Walker and
  Ian Newman, *Practical English Teaching*)

6 Student language: Assessing written work

1 The article below was written by an Italian student for a school English magazine. Read it and say what she thinks the teacher can do to keep the classroom trouble-free.

What makes a good English teacher?
Barbara Monda

NOWADAYS, for the particular role English language is playing in many fields of the modern life, English teachers are always growing in number. But, unfortunately, not all the teachers are prepared in the same way.

About myself, in two years and half at the Liceo Scientifico I have met three different English teachers, but I'm sure in the future I will think of just one of them as a good one. I think she has all the qualities, personal and professional, a good English teacher should have.

The most important thing, she has a personal interest in the students as human beings, she knows we are students, yes, but inside we are persons, with our problems and feelings, I think a good personal relation is the first thing we, students and teachers, should try to achieve, because it is an indispensable basis for a good professional relation, founded on understanding and esteem. This is very important above all in the case that students haven't chosen to study English, but are forced to because it is one of the ministerial subjects; the teacher, in this case, has to interest the students in what he or she teaches.

On my side, I can say when I went to the Liceo Scientifico I did not like English, now I study English everyday, so I cannot imagine my afternoons without it.

In three years of experience I've understood what the second most important quality for a teacher is to be well prepared and able to convey students what he/she knows. I think I don't need to explain why a teacher should be skilled. It is not unusual the fact that students at the Secondary School learn something which is completely wrong and not being particularly interested in the subject, will always persist in their mistakes. Another important point is the didactic methodologies the teacher prefers. In my opinion, a teacher should be very flexible in his/her approach: In general, I think it is better to work on pairworks, to allow students to discover things for themselves and make them free to experiment new structures, but there's also a time when a lesson with the teacher at the centre of the attention and a close comparison of the language used by students are preferable. It is the teacher who has to choose the method time by time to understand what is better for the students to improve their skills and to enjoy the lesson.

Of course, a student who likes the subject will improve his/her abilities much quicker than one who does not, but he/she has to be supported by the use of modern technologies, such as the video recorder and similar machines, with which the teacher should be familiar. At the end, for a good teacher who, since he/she does all of the things above, likes his/her job, other things that students appreciate like punctuality, marking homework and classwork on time, disponibillty to give helps outside the class-room are logical consequences.

(from Fun Press, the magazine of student work from the British Council, Naples)

---

2 If you were the editor of your school magazine, would you:

a) publish the article?
b) correct its mistakes before publication?
c) publish it uncorrected?
d) get the writer to correct it before publication?

7 Writing: A magazine article

Write an article in reply to the one above. Write about 'What makes a good English teacher/student/lesson' and refer to the article above.

8   Classroom instructions: Introducing pair correction

1 A teacher might ask a class to carry out pair correction on Section 3, Activity 1 on pages 104–5 with the instructions below. Read them and then fill in the blanks.

> 'Right, (a) .... you all finished? Have you all decided (b) .... each blank? Yes? OK. Now, let's move on to (c) .... your answers. I'd like you to correct your work (d) .... pairs, so, you look at your answer to the first blank, compare it (e) .... your partner's answer and then decide together what the answer is. Your answers may both be right, they may both be wrong, or one may be right and the other wrong. But in any (f) .... I want you to talk (g) .... your answers and discuss why you've put the answer you have. Then when you've done blank (a) go (h) .... and do blank (b) in the same way. If you can't agree (i) .... something you can ask me.
>
> 'So, remember, lots of discussion – I don't want you just to say "yes/no", "agree/disagree", but really discuss why you've put what you put. OK, does (j) .... understand?'

2 Now explain to a partner how to do pair correction as if you were speaking to a class. Use your own words or those above.

9   Conclusions

1 Teaching-related vocabulary

In one minute make a list of any words you associate with 'Trouble in the Classroom'. Compare your list with a partner.

2 Reflections on teaching

- Read 'The Six Questions' below, which are adapted from some questions devised by a British university as a framework for evaluating lessons.

What were the students/learners doing?	Was it worthwhile?
What were they learning?	What have I learned?
What was I doing?	What am I going to do next?

  During the next week evaluate your lessons with your favourite class using these questions. Then during the following week, evaluate your lessons with your least favourite class in the same way. Compare results.

- Record a lesson and then note down all the praise and criticism that you gave your students. How much praise did you give compared with criticism? How did your reactions affect your students?

14 Gender and the classroom

1 Starter activities

1 Look at the photograph and then write some adjectives you associate with girls or boys or both.

Compare and discuss your answer with a partner.

2 Look at the chart below. The verbs in the left-hand column are all actions you may do in class. Do you do some more often with male students or female students? Complete the chart with ticks in the appropriate places.

Teacher's actions	More with male students	More with female students
Praise		
Tell off		
Talk to		
Ask questions to		
Shout at		
Help		
Punish		
Ask to help you		
Ask to advise you		

Discuss your answers with a partner. Have you learnt anything about your attitudes to gender?

2   Listening

1 You're going to listen to Timothy, below, aged five, talking about the differences between boys and girls. What do you think he will think about the characteristics listed below? Listen and check your predictions. Tick the ones you made correctly.

Who are . . .?	Girls	Boys
faster		
cleverer		
stronger		
nicer		
more talkative		
gentler		
better behaved		

2 What else did you learn about Timothy?

3 Listen again. What reasons does Timothy give for:

a) playing with boys?
b) thinking girls and boys are different?
c) thinking boys are stronger?
d) thinking girls are gentler?

4 Timothy makes a number of 'language mistakes'. What are they? Do your students make similar mistakes in English? Should Timothy be corrected?

5 Talking points

Talk about one or two of the points below with a partner or partners.

Timothy at the age of five seems to believe quite strongly that girls and boys are different.

• Would five-year-old boys in your country agree with him?

• What do you think five-year-old girls might say on this subject?

• Do you think there are real differences between the sexes at this age?

3   Grammar: Tag questions; indirect questions

Tag questions

1 Listen to some excerpts from the interview with Timothy. Listen to the way in which Timothy checks the interviewer's agreement. What grammatical and intonational patterns does he follow?

2 Listen again and repeat the sentences.

3 Ask a partner some questions to check with them about personal details that you're not sure of, for example, 'You're not married, are you?', etc.

Indirect questions

4 Can you remember what the interviewer asked Timothy? Use the prompts below to help you make sentences as in the example.

age

She asked/inquired/wanted to know how old he is/was.

a) names of friends   f) nicer
b) people he plays with   g) more talkative
c) faster   h) gentler
d) cleverer   i) better behaved
e) stronger

5 How do you make indirect questions in English? Explain this to a partner as you might to a class of intermediate secondary-school students.

4   Speaking

1 Read the statements below. Are they true or false? Mark them with a T or F. Then discuss your answers with a partner.

a) Girls are gentler than boys.
b) Girls are more hard-working than boys.
c) Boys are livelier than girls.
d) Men are more conservative than women.
e) Women are more conscientious than men.
f) Women are stronger than men.

5   Student language: Assessing oral communication

1 You are going to listen to two students – an Italian man and a Japanese woman – discussing gender. They have classified the adjectives below into three groups, and are discussing their answers. Listen and complete the chart below with their opinions.

intelligent   shy   beautiful

careful

strong   loving   sweet   rough

logical

gentle   kind   hard-working

	Italian male student	*Japanese female student*
Adjectives for males	*strong*	
Adjectives for females		
Adjectives for both		

2 Which of the two students is the better communicator? Why?

3 Which of the following does each of these students master best? Number them from 1 to 5 (1 = best) for each student.

	Italian male student	*Japanese female student*
Pronunciation		
Grammar		
Vocabulary		
Fluency		
Interaction		

4 Would you be pleased or disappointed if students of yours were able to hold a conversation of this level after studying English for four years?

6　**Reading**

1 Read the magazine article below. Think of a title for it.

The girls in Jill Gugisberg Wall's science class at Farnsworth Elementary School in St Paul, Minnesota, get angry when they think about the bad old days. At the schools they attended before coming to Farnsworth, 'the boys got all the attention,' says Carrie Paladie, 12. 'Every time *we* asked a question, the teacher would just ignore us.' Her classmate, 11-year-old Jennie Montour, agrees: 'The boys got to participate in everything.' Jennie says the teachers made her feel 'that I was stupid.' Their new science teacher's mission is to change all that. 'In my classroom,' she says, 'I encourage everyone to be involved.'

Unfortunately, there are too few teachers like Wall. Sexism may be the most widespread and damaging form of bias in the classroom, according to a report released last week by the American Association of University Women. The report, which summarized 1,331 studies of girls in school, describes a pattern of downward intellectual mobility for girls. The AAUW found that girls enter first grade with the same or better skills and ambitions as boys. But, all too often, by the time they finish high school, 'their doubts have crowded out their dreams.'

In elementary school, the researchers say, teachers call on boys much more often and give them more encouragement. Boys frequently need help with reading, so remedial reading classes are an integral part of many schools. But girls, who just as often need help with math, rarely get a similar chance to sharpen their skills. Boys get praised for the intellectual content of their work while girls are more likely to be praised for neatness. Boys tend not to be penalized for calling out answers and taking risks; girls who do the same are reprimanded for being rude. Research indicates that girls learn better in cooperative settings, where students work together, while boys learn better in competitive settings. Yet most schools are based on a competitive model. The report also indicates that schools are becoming more tolerant of male students sexually harassing female students.

Despite these problems, girls get better grades and are more likely to go on to college, according to the report. But even these successful girls have less confi-

Illustration by Julia Gorton

dence in their abilities than boys, have higher expectations of failure and more modest aspirations. The result, the report concludes, is that girls are less likely to reach their potential than boys.

The differences between the sexes are greatest in science. Between 1978 and 1986, the gap between the national science achievement test scores of 9- and 13-year-old boys and girls widened – because girls did worse and boys did better. Girls and boys take about the same number of science courses, but girls are more likely to take advanced biology and boys are more likely to take physics and advanced chemistry. Even girls who take the same courses as boys and perform equally well on tests are less likely than boys to choose technical careers. A Rhode Island study found that 64 per cent of the boys who had taken physics and calculus in high school were planning to major in science or engineering, compared with only 18.6 per cent of the girls who had taken those courses.

More than two-thirds of the nation's teachers are women. Presumably, their gender bias is unintentional but no less apparent. ... 'When researchers have asked teachers to remember their favorite students, it always ends up being kids who conformed to gender stereotypes,' says researcher David Sadker. 'The ones they like best are assertive males and the ones they like least are assertive females.' ...

Keith Geiger, president of the National Education Association, the largest teachers' union, advocates incorporating gender awareness into teacher training and classroom reviews. Also, he says, as schools upgrade their math and science standards, they should encourage more participation by girls. A more controversial solution might be single-sex schools or sex segregation at crucial points in a girl's development. ...

In Jill Wall's class, girls get a lot of support from their teacher. Wall learned more about teaching girls after receiving an AAUW fellowship in 1990 during which she studied elementary science education. ... At Farnsworth, her students give her straight A's. 'She treats us all the same,' says Tamika Aubert, 11. Equity in the classroom won't turn all girls – or boys – into physicists. But maybe a generation of teachers will emerge who can delight in assertive girls and shy boys with a talent for the arts.

(from *Newsweek*)

2   Look at the words and expressions below from the article. Explain the meaning of each to a partner as you would to a group of advanced students.

to get all the attention (paragraph 1, line 8)
to ignore (paragraph 1, line 11)
sexism (paragraph 2, line 2)
remedial (paragraph 3, line 6)
to get praised (paragraph 3, lines 11–12)
to be penalised (paragraph 3, lines 15–16)
to be reprimanded (paragraph 3, line 18)
assertive (paragraph 6, line 12)
gender awareness (paragraph 7, lines 4–5)
single-sex schools (paragraph 7, lines 11–12)

3   Read the article again and note down:

a)   eight ways in which teachers are said to encourage boys more than girls.
b)   three ways in which girls show their lack of belief in themselves.
c)   three remedies suggested to counter sexism in the classroom.

Then compare your answers with a partner.

4   **Talking points**

Look at the notes you have made about how American teachers are said to encourage boys more than girls. Then talk about one or both of the points below with a partner or partners.

- Is the same true of teachers' behaviour in your country?

- Does your country's school system favour boys?

7   Writing: A magazine article

Write an article of about 250 words for an educational magazine about the treatment of boys and girls in schools in your country and the achievements of men and women. Then display your article for colleagues to read. Read your colleagues' articles and discuss them.

8 Classroom instructions: Introducing a gap-filling activity

1 At the end of each unit in this book you are asked to do a gap-filling activity like the one below. A teacher might introduce such an activity with these instructions. Read them and then fill in the blanks.

> 'OK, now I'm going to give out a passage, but it's a passage (a) .... a difference. It's not complete: it's got (b) .... in it. Now, each blank (c) .... to one missing word and what I want you to do is (d) .... in the missing words. Do you understand what you've got to do? Cristina, can you (e) .... to the others? . . . Yes, that's right. Now, to be able to fill in the blanks, don't just (f) .... Read the words before and after the blank and decide what meaning the word must (g) .... and also what part of speech it must be, (h) .... example, a noun or a preposition or an adjective, etc., etc.
>
> 'OK, you can work in (i) .... so you can talk (j) .... your answers as you go along. Is that all clear? OK, I'll just (k) .... out the passage. Cristina, could you help me, please? Thanks.'

2 Now introduce this activity to a partner as if you were speaking to a class. Use your own words or those above.

9 Conclusions

1 Teaching-related vocabulary

Look again at the article on page 114 and note in the chart below class-room behaviour/activities mentioned there that occur or do not occur in your classes. Then discuss your answers with a partner.

Occur in my classes	Do not occur in my classes
The boys get all the attention.	

2 Reflections on teaching

- Are there any ways in which you favour or discourage particular groups in your class (gender, personality type, etc.)? List them.
- Would it be helpful to change any of these ways? How?

Discuss your answers with a partner.

15 Your free time

1 Starter activities

1 Look at the photographs. What pastimes are these objects used for?

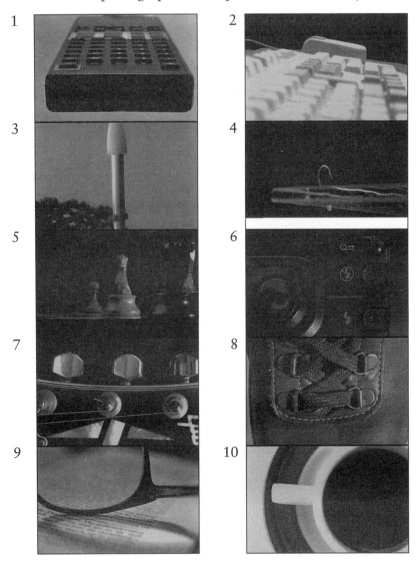

1

2

3

4

5

6

7

8

9

10

2 Do you enjoy any of these pastimes? Do you have any particular hobbies? Talk about them with a partner.

3 Read the clue below and guess the activity it describes.

> You usually do this in the evening or at night, sitting or lying down. You can do it alone or in company. Lots of people do it. You need an electric box to do it.

Now make up similar clues to describe various hobbies or spare-time activities and then ask your partner(s) to guess what they are.

2   Listening

1 Look at the chart below. You are going to listen to the four people listed there talking about two topics. Listen and decide what the topics are, and write them in the chart as headings.

Then compare and discuss your answers with a partner.

2 Now listen again and, in note form, complete the chart. Then compare your answers with a partner.

Vanessa		
Rod		
Derek		
Sue		

3 Talking points

Talk about one or two of the points below with a partner or partners.

- Which (if any) of the above people are you most/least like?
- Do these British and Australian people spend their free time in the same way as people in your country?
- How do your students generally spend their free time?

3   Writing: A first letter to a penfriend

You have arranged for your class to have some English penfriends, and you are now preparing them to write their first letter to their penfriends.

First, write a letter yourself to an imaginary penfriend so that your class can use your letter as a model for their own letters. Use the outline as a guide.

	Your address *Date*

Dear _____

This is my first letter to you and I am very pleased that you can be my penfriend.

Let me tell you something about myself:

Describe yourself

_____
_____

Describe your family

_____
_____
_____

Describe your hobbies and how you spend your time

_____
_____
_____
_____
_____

Ask your penfriend about him/herself

_____
_____
_____
_____

I hope you will be able to write back soon. I'm really looking forward to hearing from you.

Yours

4   Reading

1 Look at the article below and read the headline and the caption below the photograph. What do you think the article is about?

Playaholic's frantic fun courts death

AFTER the workaholic, alcoholic and sexaholic comes ... the playaholic.

Psychologists say it is the syndrome in which the fast-paced business executive schedules his or her 'play' activities so intensively the stress is as great as at work.

In fact it can be even greater, because 'overstructured leisure,' as business training consultant Jim Storan calls it, gets in the way of true relaxation or recreation.

'Playaholics feel guilty about time off,' he says, 'and take a mobile phone on the golf course or a portable fax on holiday.

Suffers

'And too often, in the end, the prolonged stress gets to them and their health suffers.'

President Bush was an example during the Gulf War, on the running track yet directing the Allied campaign. A less punishing routine might have spared him his heart trouble.

Clients at Priority Management, Ltd, of which Mr Storan is UK director, are taught how to stop pushing themselves so

KEEPING FIT: but to the playaholic sport is as dangerously stressful as work

hard and to make time for quiet, contemplative periods.

'Apart from their health, the executives have problems with their families, because there is no time for real relaxed communication.

'And at the end of the day, they are not necessarily any more valuable to their employers.'

His course advises applying management techniques

to personal lives – for example, writing a three-year strategic plan so as to identify what is important; things of lasting value like family celebrations.

'We had an executive tell us of a fishing trip with his son. Before they were down the drive, the boy was crying. He thought it would be cancelled yet again.'

The workaholic-playaholic syndrome is fuelled by an addiction to the get-up-and-go hormone noradrenalin, according to Dr Malcolm Carruthers, director of London's Positive Health Centre.

Effort stimulates production of the hormone, which 'tickles up pleasure centres in the brain'.

One of his patients, a retired millionaire and former workaholic, has now, he says, become 'a card-carrying playaholic: motor racing, skiing, jumping out of helicopters.

'But he is not well. At 50 he is developing heart trouble – which killed his father. I must teach him to listen to what his body is frantically trying to say.'

(from: *Sunday Express*)

2 Read the article to check your answer in Activity 1. Then complete this sentence:

A playaholic is somebody who . . .

Compare and discuss your answers with a partner.

3 Read the article again and complete the sentences. Then discuss your answers with a partner.

a) For playaholics relaxation can be more .... than work.
b) Playaholics feel .... about taking time off.
c) Priority Management is a firm which tries to .... playaholics.
d) The results of being a playaholic are .... , poor .... and poor ....
e) Playaholics are .... to the hormone noradrenalin. This stimulant is produced in the brain by ....
f) Priority Management advises its clients to prioritise things in their .... lives.

4 Look at the words and expressions below from the article. Without looking at the article again, put them into two groups: those associated with stress, and those associated with free time.

to push yourself	to get to you	fast-paced
relaxation	time off	effort
intensive	leisure	recreation
contemplative	punishing	

5 Talking points

Talk about one or two of the points below with a partner or partners. What advice, if any, would you give to your partner(s)?

- Do you play harder than you work?

- Do you feel guilty about taking time off?

- Do you think about work during your free time?

- Do you take work everywhere with you?

- Do you cancel family events for work reasons?

5   Grammar: Some modal verbs

1 You are going to write some rules for the guidance of playaholics under these headings:

a) What is necessary
b) What is unnecessary
c) What is advisable
d) What is unadvisable
e) What is allowed
f) What is compulsory
g) What is forbidden

First, match the modal verbs below with the headings.

may	should	ought to
mustn't	shouldn't	have to
ought not to	must	
need to	needn't	

2 Now write your rules for guidance, for example:

You should stop pushing yourself.

Compare your rules with a partner.

6 Student language: Assessing oral communication

1 Listen to two students – a Japanese woman and a Spanish man – talking about their leisure activities. Do they have any leisure activities in common?

2 Listen again and note down six pronunciation mistakes. (These can be mistakes in intonation, stress or sounds.)

3 If these were your students talking, would you correct their pronunciation mistakes? If you would, when would you do so and how?

7 Speaking

1 Read the statements below about free time and decide if you agree with them. Write 0, 1 or 2 next to each (2 = agree, 1 = it depends, 0 = disagree). Then compare your answers with a partner.

a) The best free-time activity is chatting with friends and family.
b) Parents never have any free time.
c) Teachers don't get enough free time.
d) Only people in rich countries have free time.
e) Time for oneself is a privilege rather than a necessity.

2 Language functions

Read the expressions below. What do they all have in common?

first of all	for another	what's more
for one thing	firstly	and on top of that
in the first place	then	in the second place

3 Compare and discuss your opinions on the statements in Activity 1, using as many of the expressions in Activity 2 as you find appropriate.

8 Classroom instructions: Introducing a discussion activity

1 A teacher might introduce the discussion activity in Section 7, Activity 1 on page 122 with the instructions below. Read them and then fill in the blanks.

'Right, in Section 7, Activity 1 on page 122 you'll (*a*) .... five statements. All of them express an opinion. Maybe you'll agree with this opinion or maybe you won't, or maybe you'll think it (*b*) .... depends. So the first (*c*) .... is to find out what you think of these opinions. I want you to read (*d*) .... the statements and write a 2 after them if you agree with them, a 0 if you disagree and a 1 if you think it depends.

'OK, now have you done (*e*) .... ? Has everyone finished? All right, now the next thing is to see if you agree with one (*f*) .... Could you get into pairs and (*g*) .... what you've put? If you don't agree with one another, give your reasons for your opinions and discuss what you think. Maybe you can make your partner (*h*) .... their mind.'

2 Now introduce the same activity to a partner as if you were speaking to a class. Use your own words or those above.

9 Conclusions

1 Teaching-related vocabulary

The vocabulary in this unit has not been about teaching. However, it contains vocabulary you might use with your classes. Read through the unit and list at least six words which one of your classes might want to learn. Discuss your choices, giving reasons.

2 Reflections on teaching

- Many units in coursebooks are (like this one) based on topics. Is it useful to base teaching and learning round a topic?
- What are the good things about topic-based materials? And the weak ones?
- How can you get round the weak points?

Tapescripts

Unit 1

4 Student language

1

Woman:
Oh if, if you can (*mm*) um what hobbies you would like to start?

Man:
Yes, I like er so much the, to play the piano (*ah, play piano*), it is one of my, my dreams (*dream, ah your dream, ah, yes*) because when I listen (*yes*) the piano music (*yes*) I, I imagine, I imagine a lot of things (*ah*) beautiful things (*yes, ah I see*) a um I like so much the, the piano (*play piano*) play the piano (*yes*). And you?

W: Um, yes, er, I want to, I want to learn (*to learn*) to dance (*to dance*) um flamenco (*flamenco*) yes (*Spanish flamenco*) yes flamenco. When I finish my school I maybe, I'll go to Spain (*mm*) to learn (*to learn flamenco*) yeah, yes flamenco (*mm*) yes and then . . . would, would you like to (*laughter*) next, would you like to play wind-surfing?

M: No, I don't like nothing, the, the sea sports because I like so much the sea but er I have er I have terror to the, I have terror in the sea (*terror*) terror, yes. I like nothing more than to see the sea (*yes*) um I don't like er swimming (*to play ah, I see*) in the sea, (*just looking*) just looking (*yes, I see*), or maybe, maybe in ten or, ten or twenty metres, nothing more (*ah, I see*). I don't like, I like for example er collect stamps (*ah, collect stamps?*), yes (*I hate it! I can't, I can't collect*) yes (*I always give up, give up to collect stamps*), yes, I like, why not (*oh, that is good*) yeah, and you have er you would have a good collection in the future yes (*yes, yes*) maybe. And I play an instruments too.

W: No I can't, I can't, I can't play anything, any instrument (*yeah*) even piano (*mm*). So how about you? (*yeah*) Could you, can you play —

M: No, I play nowaday the guitar nothing more (*guitar, oh it's good*) yeah, the Spanish guitar (*yes, oh it's lovely*) the sound is lovely.

W: Yes, yes, one day (*yeah*) please, please play the guitar for me.

M: Of course (*yeah*), of course.

5 Listening

1

Bruno and Booee speak to each other quite a bit, although talk of food dominates their conversation. At the moment, their conversations are mostly one-way: Booee will ask Bruno for a raisin, and Bruno will run away to gobble it down. Representative of these conversations were Booee's requests for orange juice: 'Gimme food drink . . . gimme drink . . . Bruno gimme.' A typical conversation for a five-year-old.

These conversations may seem unremarkable to you – no more than any typical conversation between two young children, you may think. But the conversations are in fact very remarkable. They took place between two chimpanzees who communicated with one another using the language 'Ameslan'.

Ameslan is a sign language for the deaf. Each gesture in Ameslan is made up of cheremes or basic signal units, similar to phonemes in spoken language. In all, Ameslan has 55 cheremes. It also has a grammar that organises gestures into sentences, although that grammar is significantly different from English grammar.

Bruno and Booee are just two of the many chimpanzees who have been taught Ameslan as part of an experiment to see if language is unique to humans. Ally is another of these chimpanzees. Ally has a vocabulary of 90 words, although he is only three. He picks up new signs daily, and his gestures have almost textbook clarity.

Last winter, three investigators made an explicit effort to teach Ally ten words in both English and Ameslan. First, they taught him a word in English, by saying, for example, 'Bring me the spoon'. When Ally correctly selected the spoon five consecutive times from among a variety of objects, it was assumed he reliably knew the word. When Ally knew all ten words in English, the list was divided into two sections and training began. One investigator would teach Ally the Ameslan equivalent of one of the five English words in one section. For instance, he would say 'spoon' and make the appropriate Ameslan gesture. Ally eventually demonstrated that he knew all the objects' signs in Ameslan.

While it had been known previously that Ally could acquire signs in Ameslan, in this case Ally learned the appropriate Ameslan word for a variety of objects solely on the basis of his knowledge of the English word.

Here Ally may be demonstrating that the block preventing the chimpanzee from speaking is not neurological but phonological, that is, the chimpanzee lacks the necessary mechanisms for generating and controlling particular sounds.

(adapted from *Apes, Men and Language*: Eugene Linden)

Unit 2

2 Listening

1

Emmah:

Well, mainly I've only learnt French and that is at school for the last five years and, um but primarily when I went abroad on a school trip to France for three weeks I learnt mostly a lot of French then.

Interviewer:

Um and um what about how you learnt French at school? I mean do you think you, you learnt in a good way? Do you think you could have learnt in any better ways?

E: Well, I learnt, yes I did learn a lot because I passed my exam but I do think that the way in which we were taught was, well to me, I could have found easier ways such as more conversation and less actual written work because it's conversation that's going to be needed more than anything else.

I: What sort of, I mean you say you had lots of written work, um what kind of written work and do you think you got anything out of that?

E: Um well, we had a lot of grammar to learn, and like verbs, verb tables to just learn off by heart and that kind of thing, trying to incorporate that in conversation I find it very difficult whereas where we had, where we did have conversations um we just like picked up the verbs and the grammar on the way which was a lot easier.

I: And when you were at school learning French did you have much opportunity for conversation in French?

E: No, not really, it was mostly um working from textbooks and we didn't have a lot of conversation-based um lessons at all.

I: OK. Right, now that's talked a little bit about when you were learning French at school. What, what sort of a way do you think you'd really like to learn?

E: I would enjoy um having pure French conversations throughout the classes and then having to write essays on, for example, what we talked about or a subject that we talked about and then from there I could learn the grammar or read out our essays and learn the grammar from there.

I: But, no, you wouldn't like, you wouldn't like any sort of formal grammar input, you'd like to just sort of pick it up?

E: Um I don't know because I guess it is necessary but I would feel it a lot easier if I were to pick it up along the way.

I: Yeah, and what about vocabulary?

E: Um that too, if we just had um phrase books and, and um dictionaries with us I'm sure we would have been able to get along fine.

I: Instead of which, what were you, what did you do?

E: Just as I said before, just um learning directly from textbooks and not learning anything that was, um say words that the everyday French people speak, just um proper words, no slang, no, no getting on with French um everyday talk, language.

I: Right. And in an ideal world, I mean you know with or without the classroom, how do you think, what for you would be the best way to learn a language?

E: To ultimately live in the country or spend time in that, um, particular country for a couple of months.

Unit 3

5 Student language

1

Alberto:

Er, what do you doing in er November 24th of er (*1988*) two years ago, three years ago?

Maki:

Two years ago, yes, um this day I was er I going to my high school (*um*) and um I belonged to um English drama club. Maybe I, um I did exercise too, yes, but I'm not sure. (*in the morning, in the morning*) Morning!

A: No, I ask you in the morning (*ah yeah*) you, you go, you went to the school.

M: Yes, yes that's right.

A: Um, me (*mm*), um at 24 (*what are you doing, yes?*) I, I went to, is my birthday (*ah, is your birthday, oh*), yes, birthday and er is, was important for me because er (*yes*) when um in this years I, I was er eighteen years old (*mm*) and for me very important because er I like very much er to do um in um in um by car and er when (*it's present!*) yes, yes for, for my, my present was a car.

M: Oh, it's great present.

A: Yes, very great present. (*laughter*)

M: I see. And um did you, did you get a present anything else for your friends er and parents?

A: Oh yes, yes but er for me it was very important the car.

M: Ah! (*laughter*) Yes I understand…um, yes. 6 of April 91, um that day I um depart, I departed in my country (*ah yeah*) to in England to here, it's that day start er my new, new life.

A: I understand. I um in the 6th of April I went to

my grandmother's er house (*yes*) for er to welcome (*mm*) for my, for my depart (*yes*) to um to, to England to, to come here (*I see*) for my, also with my, my, my parent, my, my, my cousin (*I see*), yeah.

6 Listening

2

Clare Boylan:

I had very little rural experience in my childhood at all. We were Dubliners, we were kids who played in the lane and um went to the movies and ate chips.

I was the youngest and at various stages um my elder sister, three years older than me, was a 'twin' to me, and at other stages she was a 'twin' to my older sister. And um, we were very, very close. Um we circled around each other like little moths in motes of dusty light.

Edna O'Brien:

There was an avenue up from, from the road, and it was a big house. I mean, looking at it now it's not quite as big as it seemed to one then, but it was big, it had about five bed-rooms, it had um, as I say, this drive up to it, and then a second gate that led into the front of the house, and when the sun shone I used to think that it was a kind of heaven. And it was very beautiful.

Dervla Murphy:

I didn't really make any close childhood friends because I liked going off in the morning, and I mean this was in the school holidays, cycling off with a few books in the carrier, and finding a nice place to settle down and read them.

Maeve Binchy:

I have a very firm earliest memory, and I was three and a half, and at that stage my mother was expecting another child, but I didn't obviously understand a thing like this, but I was constantly adding to my prayers, you know, apart from praying, 'God bless Mummy and Daddy' and all that, 'Please send me a new brother or sister'. And it seemed like, you know, I got the word 'me' in it – 'Please send me' – and I thought 'That's great', 'cos I loved things that were given to me, things to open, parcels and presents, and I was outraged when it arrived, because the whole attention shifted from me to this small red-faced thing in a cot, and I said to my mother apparently, I remember looking at it, and my first memory is looking at it with great disappointment because this was something I'd been praying for, and this thing wailing and wailing and everyone saying wasn't it beautiful, and I said, 'To be frank,' (*I don't*

suppose I used the words 'To be frank'), but I said, 'But honestly, I'd really prefer a rabbit.'

Unit 4

2 Listening

1

Man 1:

I think I started to learn English about twenty, no 30 years ago, almost 30 years ago, and as far as I can remember the coursebook was very theoretical, um there was a text and after the text there were some questions on the text, then we talked about grammar problems in this lesson and afterwards we did grammar exercises but I can't remember any communicative activity, any dialogue, any conversation, any interaction.

Man 2:

There was an interaction – the teacher asking 'What have you learned?' (*laughter*)

M1: Yeah, but between the teacher and the pupil only and never between pupils.

Woman:

And don't forget the vocabulary which was very important too (*mm*) and which still should be important.

M2: Just a list of English words (*and German*) and a list of German words and one English word for one German word (*yes*).

M1: There were no synonyms, no definitions, no opposites, no gaps. (*no collocations*) It helped me to learn a lot *about* the language, about English, about the system of the language, but one year after I left high school I went to London for the first time and I couldn't under-stand anybody, it was even difficult for me to, to just to buy things because I read a lot in English, I could read the newspaper but I had no experience in, in listening and in, in communi–, in talking to English people, the only voice I heard at school was the voice of my teacher, we never had a cassette with a native speaker.

W: We were very good in translating texts I think because we really knew the German meaning of each word (*mm*) and now they often only have a vague impression of the German meaning because in our lessons now we don't refer to the German expression very often.

M1: Mm. The language during the lessons was more or less German and not English (*exclusively*). The big difference (*exclusively, only the reading was in English*) yeah, yeah.

W: I can't remember any communication practice
    at all. We never had a given situation where we
    tried to practise a dialogue or things like that.

M2: That's, that, but as you said, we were very,
    very good at translating English and
    philosophical texts, political texts, and —

M1: Yes, we knew a lot about, about the political
    system, about the history, the geography of, of
    Great Britain and the USA.

Unit 5

5 Listening

1

Man:
       I think, I think a good lesson, really um I think
       the main thing is that it should be fun and it
       should be interesting. Um. I think those, I think
5   those are some of, some of the main points
       about a lesson.

Woman 1:
       Do you think fun is really important?

M: Um I think they should be, yeah, I think, I think
10   when I say 'fun' I mean um that the students
       should be able to enjoy themselves and, um,
       thereby feel relaxed, you know.

Woman 2:
       Maybe we could say that if the students feel
15   really involved, um, even if they're not actually
       having 'fun'.

M: Yeah, I mean, I don't mean you have to play
     games and stuff every lesson, um but I think a
     certain amount of games and playing, yeah, um
20   reduces tension in the classroom and is good.

W2: And I often find that if you're teaching students
    that have been used to um a very passive
    methodology like the Taiwanese, if you
    introduce this element of fun they respond
25 quite well to it, because they are fairly bored
    with the way they've been taught although
    they expect, they sort of expect to be taught
    that way but they are quite open to doing
    something completely different.

30 W1: And they do realise quite quickly that they are
    doing something linguistically as well, don't
    they, even if they start off the first lesson or the
    second lesson, by the third lesson they realise
    what they're doing by and, as you say, they enjoy
35 it (*yeah*), they're quite happy to do it. (*Yeah. So
    . . .*)

W2: And also, so I suppose there's also, the other
    thing is difference in pace in the lesson, you've
    got to, you can't *keep* doing the same thing so
40 you can't *keep* playing games and you can't (*oh

yeah, sure) *keep* them sitting at their desks so
you want, you want to vary the activities that
you use so that there is, there are moments
when they're doing something that's quiet and
maybe just spending some time um thinking   45
about something and other times when
they're working together or working as a whole
class, so as long as you keep um a variety. And I
think it's also very important that they go away
feeling that they've done something (*right*),   50
that they've learnt something, achieved
something, so as well as the element of, even if
it is a lesson where there is a tremendous
element of fun and everyone was laughing, at
least when they go away they have some sort   55
of feeling that 'Well, we've done something in
this lesson'.

M: Yeah, I mean, I think really one of the, yeah,
     another main thing about a good lesson, the
     students must learn something, but yeah, like   60
     you say, they, they have to see that they've
     learnt something.

W1: Mm. So you also need a very clear idea really,
    don't you, of what you are going to do with
    them (*right*) and you've got to be very sure   65
    when you go in of the kind of direction that
    you're going to go in.

M: I think you need, I think you need goals and I
     think they need goals as well, um you know I
     mean very often they need to see why they're   70
     doing, you know, why they're doing this piece
     of work, you know, if they can see a value to it,
     if they see 'OK, this is why we are doing it' then
     it's not so bad, you know, they, they at least
     know what they're doing.   75

Unit 6

2 Listening

1

My first job was an utterly disastrous experience. I
only stayed a week, because the headmaster hated
me and I hated him. He came into my room about
every ten minutes or so and kept saying, 'Why aren't
they writing in ink? Why aren't they doing joined-up
writing? Why aren't they doing harder sums?' And
there was I with 40 tough little kids trying to get on
top of them. I'm not saying that there weren't faults
on my side, but it was a very unnerving experience.
On the Thursday I rang the education office and said
that I couldn't stay there. The head had apparently
rung the office too.

So, on Friday, the inspector arrived. It was a very
amusing experience. He came into the room and had

a few fatherly words with me and said, 'I'll show you how to control the class.' He clapped his hands and started to talk, but the children just called out ribald remarks. They really were tough little kids. So he quickly realised that he wasn't going to be able to do anything with them, certainly not show off to a younger teacher. As he fled, he turned in the doorway and said, 'I'll ring you from the office.' And sure enough I got a phone call later telling me to report to the office on Monday. I was sent to another school where I settled down happily.

I feel that education is absolutely a three-way partnership, if you can have such a thing, between the child, the parent and the teacher. There's no valid argument for denying parents the chance to be involved. We send reading books home regularly. I have parents in to hear children read, though not to teach them. And on odd occasions I might have parents in to help with cookery. Considering their expressed concern about their children's education, not nearly as many parents volunteer as you might think.

The atmosphere in my classroom is all-important to me. I work very hard to create a good relationship between the children and myself, which doesn't mean that I give in to them. I'm regarded as very strict, but I feel children need that firmness to feel safe. Sometimes I shout at them. I always feel ashamed afterwards. I encourage the class to discuss discipline. If there's been an epidemic of aggression in the playground, for example, instead of talking to the offender in the corner, I discuss it in front of the class. I think it's good for the offender to hear what other children think about his behaviour.

My greatest stress is having too little time to achieve what I want. I also find it stressful if colleagues are inadequate because that puts a great strain on everybody else. Some teachers do the absolute minimum and have no real interest in the children at all.

I don't want to sound terribly pious about myself, but I really do hope every week that I shall reach the children and see some of them grow a bit. Sometimes, however, I just think, 'Oh, God! Monday! It's raining.'

(from *Teachers*: Frank E. Hugget)

6 Student language

2
Woman:
    Yes, out which of er this relationships er are most important for you?
Man:
    Mm, it's er parents.
W: Parents, why?
M: Because I think er they are the most close

people to me or to everyone in the world because you know from the beginning, from the first day you are born, they look after you and they all the time keeping you safe, er they give you what you want, everything you need, they, it's really for you, they make really for you.
W: Yes, I agree with you, the parents all the times must be important for us, yes you are right and er I think the least important er relationship is others, no, neighbours. What do you think?
M: No, neighbours I think er should be the third, er the third, er position er.
W: Why?
M: Because they are close to you, maybe you live with your parents er neighbours a long time, maybe after neighbours for ten years or fifteen years and you know them well and they know you well and if you want anything or something from them or they need anything, you're all together.
W: And what do you think about boy and girl-friend?
M: Boy and girlfriend, I think it's the least er relationship. (*laughter*)
W: This is more, please.
M: Yeah, because er I think boyfriend or girlfriend sometimes they have argument or possibly change in a three years or something, it's not important to have a girlfriend or a boyfriend, it's one along your life, and you know the argument and if the girl saw her boyfriend look another girl and she be jealous or something like this (*mm*) I don't think it's the important thing in your life.
W: I think for me it's important er after the parents because er we all the times share lots of thing and we all the times together, I think it must be important.
M: There is a thing, a lot of things is more important than the boyfriend and the girlfriend.
W: Which one?
M: The other er members of your family (*yes*) is important than them. Your sisters, your brothers (*laughter*), your grandfather, mother, it's important than you have a boyfriend (*yes, but*) all that you ????????? live in the same house.

Unit 7

7 Listening

2

It seems to me that teacher development is a crucial part of every teacher's um educational improvement for one very important reason or perhaps two very important reasons.

First of all, um there is a tendency I think for all teachers to get into a rut; that is to, to fall into a very, very repetitive pattern of teaching so that you tend to do the same kinds of things over and over again. Um this is inevitable to a certain extent because like all um aspects of your life you have to do certain things in a repetitive way. I mean at a very basic level if your, if your walking skills were something that you had to learn afresh every day, life would be very hard. Similarly with teaching, an awful lot of the things that you do in the classroom you quickly learn to do automatically. When you're first teaching you don't, you have to think all the time and that's why teaching at first is very, very tiring, but after a while things become more automatic and that keeps you sane – it means that if you're teaching, say, 25, 30 lessons a week, a lot of what you do is automatic, you don't have to plan it, you don't have to think about it. However, there is a negative side to that: if all of your teaching becomes automatic or mechanical or formulaic you, um your teaching will become very dry and uninspiring. So one very, very important reason for teacher development is that it helps you to counter that ritual, formulaic side of your teaching, um, in two ways.

First of all, you are helped by whatever group of teachers you work with or by your teacher developer, you are helped to look at the things that you have become blind to – things that you have maybe a long time ago started to do completely mechanically, completely routinely. It might be something as simple as the way in which you, you hand out books to your students or the way in which you use the whiteboard or blackboard or the way in which you introduce vocabulary before a listening exercise; you may have got into a complete routine there and you have lost touch with, you haven't, you don't realise any more that you are doing it. So in teacher development you are helped to look at what you have lost touch with.

Um you're also helped to understand what lies behind what you're doing so, to take a very simple example, you may some time ago have read about or seen a demonstration of somebody doing some kind of information-gap activity where students are put in pairs or in groups and half the group or one of the pair knows, has some information, and the other half has other information and you exchange information and you, as it were, have developed a way in which you do this activity, er but the way in which you do it has, has again become mechanical and ritualised and you have forgotten completely why you are doing it; you have forgotten the principle behind it, the principle in this case that if two people are talking to each other normally, they are usually, they don't know everything, there is a gap between them, there is information that one wants to get across to the other, but very often in your classroom teaching you have lost touch with that principle. So that's the second reason for, um or the second way in which your mechanical teaching can be refreshed; the people you're working with in teacher development or your teacher developer can actually get you to see why that particular activity or technique is done and you perhaps have lost touch with that and you are able to see why you are doing it, why you should be doing that activity and once you see again why you should be doing it you are able to, perhaps, reorganise the way you do it or do it completely differently; it becomes fresh again.

Um another, a third area of teacher development which is very, very important is um bringing to the surface, so that you can actually talk about it, your tacit knowledge. It may be that you do a lot of things in class expertly; er a classic example of that might be the way in which you deal with discipline problems with children. Um, I think this is particularly so in teachers in state education who have been teaching for a long time; they have these skills and yet they are probably quite unable to articulate them, to talk about how they do it. Now that for the individual teacher may not matter very much – why should a teacher, if he does something very well, why should he or she actually be able to talk about it? But if you're in a group, a development group, a teacher development group, then it's very very, valuable to be able to share that er knowledge, that tacit knowledge with other people so that seems to be another purpose of teacher development groups – that er you are able to draw out of your peers, your colleagues, skills that they have and have never talked about before so that they can share that, that very, very, very useful information with other people.

(Peter Maingay)

Unit 8

7 *Listening*

3

Interviewer:

Right, I wonder if you could maybe say something on, about what you think makes a good teacher, the sort of characteristics of a good teacher.

Emmah:

Well, to me it doesn't matter what subject it is, it applies to all teachers. Um just so long as each teacher can put themselves on the same level as the student or the pupil that they are teaching, to be able to go back to when *they* were learning and be able to put themselves in our positions because there are lots of teachers that like I have come in contact with that get so frustrated because they know so much and they are trying to teach us and they can't remember when they were in exactly the same position so I think like empathy plays quite a large part.

I: Mm, mm. Um what about whether a teacher is sort of well trained or not; I mean what do you think is more important, a teacher's sort of personality or their knowledge of their subject or how much they know about techniques of, of teaching?

E: I think personality goes an awful long way because it doesn't matter how, well, they have to have obviously a basic teaching knowledge, but other than that as long as they're able to, um go back to the beginning and even learn again with us and be able to explain things in more detail, that's all we really need, just some one that can put themselves in our position and help us through things rather than ordering us to do things.

I: So somebody kind (*yes, definitely*), patient (*yep*); what other sort of qualities?

E: Um. Yeah, very tolerant (*mm*) and someone who obviously enjoys teaching rather than enjoys the subject that they teach in, someone who really does enjoy um coming in contact with people, it has to be someone very sociable.

I: So somebody who is able to relate more to the students than to their subject or, or equally at least.

E: At least equally, yes, so, so we can get a balanced sort of um view.

I: And you think that goes right across all subjects?

E: Yes, I do (*mm*), I do definitely.

Unit 9

2 *Listening*

1

Glo:

Yes, um well I'll start by telling you my age. I'm 49, so I've had rather a chequered career. Um at the moment I, my main interest is leading on courses on self-esteem, so I run courses on self-   5 esteem enhancement, enhancing hopefully people's self-esteem. Um I was trained actually as a landscape gardener, plants and gardening being my, my other great passion but I now do less of that and more of the self-esteem courses.   10

Interviewer:

Right. So you've already had, sort of, um made a fairly big change in, in your life.

G: Yes. A complete new direction, um certainly involving more and more people. I love to be   15 with people, I like to share, er how people tick and communicate with them, er just see where, where they are in their lives and um what they're going to do with their life. It's, it fascinates me.   20

I: And well, you've, you've already said that you're, you're 49; I mean there is a saying that life begins at 40 and, how do you feel about that?

G: (*laughter*) I think um I think my life begins   25 almost afresh um every six months um; I, I've never had the feeling that it, it went downhill after 40 um but whether it took off at 40 um maybe, maybe, maybe it did, did um in, in some respects. I think you certainly get more in touch   30 with the direction that you want to go in. The, the, the exciting thing for me is that, just to be able to keep on changing, um I've never planned anything that's happened in my life, um things have happened, opportunities have   35 come into my life and I've either said 'Yes' or 'No'.

I: So you don't feel with the passing of the years you've become more conservative or less open to change or . . .   40

G: Oh, no, no, I don't think I've been more conservative. I'd like to think I've become more eccentric um but I think I have become more open to er to change. There seems an incredible quality in, in being able to change several   45 times, if not more than that in one's life.

I: And what do you see, that quality, I mean why, why are you so interested in change? Why is it so, why do you find it so stimulating?

G: I think because it stops you being completely   50 stuck um along one direction um it's, it's energising er and just the thought of the

possibility that you can go on changing until
55   you're 75 is er is life-giving.
I: Have you any idea what you might be doing in
     ten years from now, twenty years from now?
G: No, and I don't think I'd like to know. I'd like to
     think that it's all still a mystery, though, I don't
60   know, I love what I'm doing at the moment and
     I'd like to think that I'll go on enjoying doing
     whatever it is. Um there's nothing I have to do,
     I'm lucky in that respect, er I can keep on
     choosing what I want to do and I've no idea
65   what's going to be out there for me in ten
     years' time.
I: Well, you sound all really excited by it all.

4   *Student language*

1

Takako:

    My name is Takako from Japan. I'm nineteen
    years old.

Maria:

    My name is Maria from Spain. I am twenty,
    twenty-two years old.

T: What do you think you will be like in twenty
     years' time?
M: Um I would like my life, um OK in my, in my life
     er with my family, with my husband (*mm*), my
     childrens (*mm*), maybe four childrens, three son
     and one er one daughter in a house, in my
     house in a countryside (*mm*).
T: Will you be happy?
M: Yes, of course (*laughter*) (*yes*), I think so.
T: With Paulo? Pablo?
M: With Pablo, I don't know, Takako (*laughter*)
     with who but I hope with Pablo, yes of course.
     And you?
T: Mm twenty years' time, I don't know, but
     maybe I, I will get married (*maybe*) mm. Yes, of
     course.
M: But do you want this?
T: Yes, I want get marry early, early. Um. Maybe,
     um.
M: And childrens?
T: Children, children, one or two.
M: One or two.
T: Yes.
M: Because in Japan it's very difficult, no?
T: No, no, no, no, it's OK.
M: It's OK?
T: No problem, but . . .
M: But the families er haven't got . . .
T: Only one or two or three (*yes*) mm, normally,
     yeah.
M: And the work? What do you think about the
     work (*work*) in twenty years, in twenty years?
T: Maybe no, not a lot (*no*), only housewife (*yes,*

me too, I think) and er I hope er I will go out
with my friend, I'll go out with my friend, play
tennis (*ah*), yes I hope (*a good life, OK, mm?*)
yes (*yes, OK, me too*) and my, my dream (*your
dream*) is my friend and my er have er children,
same age (*yes, yes*), a very good relationship
(*yes*) each other.
M: Ah, you, you can go to the . . .
T: My friend's house (*with your children*)
     (*laughter*).
M: Yes, yes, beautiful. My, my dreams is the same,
     (*yes*) is beautiful because I think in the future I
     prefer stay with my family and my house (*yes*)
     than work (*yes*), the same you. Go, I have my
     childrens and after er we, no I bring my children
     to the school with my friend (*mm*) and after
     go to the shopping (*yes*) yes and (*eat
     something*) look for my family (*ah, yeah*),
     look for, look after? Look for . . .

Unit 10

5   *Listening*

1

Presenter:

    Frieda Smith, a British secondary-school teacher,
    spent two weeks working in a Danish school
    and found a school life that British teachers are
    still campaigning for. Frieda went on an
    exchange trip to a *gymnasium* situated in a
    town to the north of Copenhagen. The school
    takes students from 16 to 24 hoping to go to
    university.

Frieda:

    One of the most striking features of the Danish
    system is how much better resourced they are in
    terms of staffing, equipment and buildings than
    we are in Britain. Maximum class size is set at 28
    in the *gymnasium* although many are smaller.
    Contact time is limited according to the amount
    of marking each subject requires – I taught
    seventeen, 45-minute English lessons a week.
    Teachers are under no obligation to cover for
    absences in the *gymnasium*, but if they contract
    to do cover they are paid extra whether they
    are required or not. Teachers are not obliged to
    be on the premises during non-contact time.
    The Danes still believe that teaching students
    and the preparation of lessons are the most
    important parts of a teacher's job!
P: Frieda also noticed a difference in the buildings.
F: The fabric of school buildings is far superior.
     Fixtures and fittings are of good quality.
     Windows are always double-glazed. Heating is

effective and quiet. All classrooms have curtains and blackout.

P: The *gymnasium* had approximately 70 staff to 800 students. Each class had two members of staff responsible for them and class sizes averaged around 25. The *gymnasium* was well equipped with computers, printing machinery, photocopiers, binders and typewriters.

F: Most useful was the seemingly limitless supply of paper, pens, pencils, rubbers, rulers, glue, scissors, staplers and hole-punchers. This eliminated at a stroke the lost hours in any British teacher's life as the four corners of the building are scoured for any or all of these. The differences these and other considerations – like freedom from form-filling and decent clerical support – make to morale is difficult to quantify, except that it restores one's belief that teaching really is a profession and not just a job. It's a feeling that teachers in Britain no longer share.

The exchange gave me a renewed sense of my own vocation. I remembered what it is I enjoy about teaching.

(Adapted from 'Nothing wrong in the state of Denmark': Martin Brown, *The Teacher*)

Unit 11

5 Student language

1

Woman 1:
How busy, busy is your life at home, in your country?

Woman 2:
In Japan?

W1: Yes.

W2: Um I, I go to school (*mm*) er I studied English (*yes*) er it's very difficult for me.

W1: Studying English, yes another language, another alphabet (*yeah*), I think so, but er normally you have moment for relaxing er for er free time, for example er?

W2: Yes, I have (*yes er*) um wake up er how, sorry (*laughter*) ?????? And you?

W1: Me? Is not very busy in my country (*mm*) but um I haven't, er from last October I haven't er been in my country because er I was in Germany for six months and now I'm here (*mm*) for another six months and er yes is stress because I have to study another language, it's not my language, er (*oh*) for example English was very difficult because I was only beginner yet (*mm*) and so I, er I have to study a lot of, but it's not like er for example er to work, er to work is very stress (*oh*) because you are always er in, for example

me, in an office, er you have to answer all telephone (*mm*), you have talk with people, write er a lot of er noisy (*yeah, mm*) and so on, here is very relaxing for me (*mm*) I think and I can meet a lot of people. I can speak, er it's OK I think. In my country it's not um because I live in a small town and so (*small town?*) yes, it's a very small town (*laughter*), nothing to do really but for me um work is a stress because er maybe because er I didn't like um my job, um I was secretary to, it was very boring (*oh*) and so I, I took a lot of stress (*mm, stress*) and now is a holiday for me (*laughter*), yes, a holiday for me.

W2: What did you do er, er when you be secretary?

W1: Oh, a lot of things, (*typewriter*) yes typewriter, write a computer, er I, I worked by insurance er and so I, um I had to read a lot of er book about insurance and take info–, news (*mm*) and er I had to explain a customer er about, er for example, er this insurance or this insurance (*mm*) and er was good but um maybe I, I had the chef, you know the chef, the company director not very good (*laughter*). I think he don't like me and so ooh terrible (*laughter*), yes, always angry (*laughter*) and so always er I took er a lot of stress (*oh*).

7 Listening

1

Interviewer:
Mrs Battersby, you're a teacher in an English primary school, isn't that right?

Monica:
Yes, I am.

I: Um and how many classes do you have?

M: I just have one class.

I: Right. Um. And can you tell us something about the class?

M: Um. They're a mixed class of Reception and Year 1 children so they vary from age four, five to six.

I: So Reception is the, what is Reception exactly?

M: Reception are the new children when they first start school.

I: OK. Under five.

M: Yes. Yes.

I: Um I wonder if you could say something about what it is that you're teaching or working on with the children this year?

M: Um well, the main aim that we have is to teach the children to read and number work and we do quite a lot of science, early science now, and lots of art and craft and manipulative skills (*mm*) um and we do this through project work. This year we've been doing projects on movement, weather and mini-beasts.

I: Mini-beasts? What are mini-beasts?

M: The insects and small creatures.

I: Right. (*laughter*) Um so you do project work. Does that mean you work through group work rather than whole-class work?

M: We do some and some, um I do a lot of group work but I often do class work as well when I'm talking and discussing something, we do it as a class but the actual tasks are done in groups because you can't actually get round 32 children at the same time so you have to organise your tasks, you know, so that they're doing different sorts of things.

I: And do you have any individual work as well?

M: Er, yes, I do individual work, um a morning a week when I have an extra teacher to help me.

I: It all sounds as if it means an awful lot of organisation.

M: Yes it does, a lot.

I: Well, could you maybe describe um how that organisation works out in the course of an average day or just maybe tell us how you spend your average day?

M: Um well I start at half past seven in the morning, um when I'm organising my groups, getting the apparatus ready and making paints and glue.

I: So you're actually in work at half seven?

M: Yes, yes, each day, and so I work from half seven until ten to nine when the children arrive and I spend I suppose half of my lunch hour getting group work ready for the afternoon and then I stay about an hour after school each night, sometimes longer.

I: So half seven to half four or so, your day...

M: Is an average day, yes.

I: And when you're not preparing, when you're actually sort of teaching, how does the day work out?

M: Well, we start off with um assembly and then we come back and then I talk to the children about the tasks and activities I want them to do that day and then while they're actually doing them I'm sort of moving around from group to group and then we have, we have story times just before play and just before lunch and we have P.E. times during the day and music times, as well as the language, maths and science and art activities going on all day.

I: (*laughter*) Goodness. And how about at home? Do you ever work at home?

M: Yes (*laughter*) – most evenings, and I spend quite a bit of time at the weekends as well, and at holiday time we have to organise our project for the term.

I: And do you enjoy your job?

M: Yes, I, I enjoy teaching, the actual teaching part I still enjoy, yes.

Unit 12

4 Listening

2

And in my job I have to recruit teachers to work overseas. The kinds of jobs that I recruit for are basically normally either people who are not very experienced or people who are *very* experienced and so naturally I'm looking for different qualifications and for different experience in both kinds of jobs.

If we're looking at the jobs for teachers with um very little experience then normally we will want a university degree and a, a teaching qualification, an EFL teaching qualification such as the UCLES RSA Certificate. If we're looking for people with more experience then probably we're looking for a degree, um, the UCLES RSA Diploma, maybe a master's degree in applied linguistics, something like that.

But as important as qualifications are, and you won't get to an interview or at least people won't get to an interview without the qualifications, the most important thing in fact is the character and how a person presents themselves at interview. I find it very difficult to define exactly the sort of person I am looking for, but when I meet someone I can tell whether they are the sort of person that I would like to appoint or whether they are not.

At interview the first thing that I notice is how the person settles down, when they sit down. Do they immediately rush into the room, grab a chair without being invited to sit down? Are they nervous? Um, do they spend a lot of time fiddling with their hands, brushing their hair back, er holding their pen, tapping it on the table? Obviously everyone is nervous at interview and you make allowances for that, but if it continues throughout the whole interview then of course you have to ask yourself if they're like this after, say, an hour of interview, what will they be like in a normal job?

Second thing that I look for is: Do they look at you? Do they make eye contact? Because if they won't look at *you* in a job where in, in a situation where a job depends on, on them making a good impression, then probably in the job they won't do very well in terms of making, er, good, making contact with other colleagues, making, having good relations with other colleagues. The sort of person normally we would look for would be someone who was, open, outgoing, enthusiastic and who could talk intelligently about what they had done and what they hoped to do. That doesn't mean that they have to have had a lot of experience but that they should be able to reflect on whatever experience they've had.

The other kinds of, of um things that we might

talk about in an interview of course are what, er what the person expects to get from a new job in a new country, and that I think is important because it shows the expectations that the person has – what they want from their job. Um it's interesting to hear why people want to change jobs, why they want to go to a new country.

6 Student language

1
Harako:
  Carla, (*yes*) what kind of person do you like?
Carla:
  Er, I like my teacher.
H: Uh huh. Um why do you like?
C: Because very good teacher (*mm*), extraordinary teacher, um he is very nice (*mm*), wonderful person (*mm*) and he is, er he know what er to do for students (*yes, yes*), for progress.
H: Yes, I came here England, er now um I study English and, but um teacher is very kind and English person very kind; yes, I am very happy.
C: Yes, I think er here there is everybody is very friendly (*yes, yes*) (*laughter*).
H: And what kind of person do you dislike?
C: Oh, maybe you can say?
H: I dislike person is um don't keep promise person (*yes*) so, for example, my classmate um sometime go to restaurant as ?????????? but er most of the people (*mm*) don't keep promise so if you are someone don't keep promise um, um it is very bad so, er for example, go to restaurant and we reserved er a table but everybody don't come, very problem (*mm*) so, and er, um. I dislike person is er, um mm um . . .
C: Don't worry, maybe you ?????????? to me. I think here everybody is very friendlier er as every, everyone help you, help everyone ?????????? at college (*mm, yeah*).

Unit 13

5 Listening

3
First of all you can make your classroom as attractive and as stimulating as possible. It should look orderly and purposeful and create the expectation that people do useful work here. It should also be a place that makes your work as easy as possible. The way the furniture is arranged must reflect the way you want to work. It need only take a couple of minutes for a class to rearrange their tables and chairs, after a little practice.

Your lesson planning can also help your classroom management. Plan your lessons so that the work is differentiated; so that every pupil, even the lowest attainer, has something productive that they can do and so there is a graded sequence of higher-level extension activities for the others.

Of utmost importance too is how you relate to your class. Teaching is a professional activity, requiring human warmth, tact, sensitivity, resolve and professional detachment. The management of pupils needs to be calm, patient and measured. Your comments should be as positive as possible. You should give more praise than censure, more reward than punishment. We should try to reinforce the behaviour we want more than we complain about the behaviour we don't want.

Think too about your own behaviour. Be consistent and don't let your own psychological baggage make you moody. Something ignored one day and punished the next is naturally resented by pupils. And if a situation arises which you cannot control, stay calm and send immediately for support from a senior member of staff.

And finally, don't forget: all the advice in the world can only be of limited use unless we are willing to examine and reflect on what we do in the classroom. Systematic evaluation is the key to any effective teacher development.

(adapted from 'Classroom Discipline': Clifford Walker and Ian Newman, *Practical English Teaching*)

Unit 14

2 Listening

1
Interviewer:
  Timothy. All right. And how old are you Timothy?
Timothy:
  Five and three-quarters.
I: Mm. Do you go to school?
T: Yes.
I: Mm. Are there lots of boys and girls in your class?
T: Quite a lot.
I: And can you tell me the names of some of your friends?
T: Thomas, Jamie, Thomas and Guy; Sam, um, Harry.
I: Yes?
T: That's all.
I: All of those are boys.
T: And Maria and Clare and, I don't know, I haven't got any more.

I: So you normally play with boys more than girls?
T: Yes.
I: Why's that?
T: I like boys best (*do you?*). I'm a boy, I'm a boy myself (*laughter*).
I: And do you think girls and boys are different?
T: Yes.
I: In what kind of way?
T: Um, girls, boys can't do, have babies, girls can and um, not much, um, lady polices, is there?
I: Not many lady police (*mm*). No. Do you think girls and boys are different as people?
T: Yes, why, why um men um can fight in um dangerouser ways than girls, can't they?
I: Do you think so? (*Yes, do you?*) I suppose it's true; why do you think that is?
T: Why, um, um God made it like that, didn't he?
I: Mm. And let me see, so who do you think are faster, boys or girls?
T: Um sometimes girls when they have, um when they are older (*mm*) and what else?
I: OK, who do you think's cleverer?
T: Boys sometimes.
I: And sometimes girls?
T: Yes.
I: All right. Who do you think's stronger?
T: Boys.
I: Always?
T: Of course.
I: Why of course?
T: Why they do the powerfullest fighting.
I: Mm. And who do you think's nicer?
T: The girls.
I: The girls are nicer?
T: Yes.
I: And why are the girls nicer?
T: Why they are.
I: And who talks more, boys or girls?
T: Girls.
I: And who do you think is gentler?
T: Um of course girls are nicer, girls, girls are nice so, so girls won't fight, (*mm*) will they?
I: I don't know.
T: Some do, don't they?
I: But not really?
T: No.
I: They're much, they're, they're more gentle, are they? Who's better behaved, boys or girls?
T: Girls are better behaved.
I: Do you think so?
T: Yes.
I: OK.

3 Grammar

1
a) Not much lady polices, is there?
b) Men can fight in dangerouser ways than girls, can't they?
c) God made it like that, didn't he?
d) Girls are nice, so girls won't fight, will they?
e) Some do. don't they?

5 Student language

1
Woman:
    What, what do you think strong?
Man:
    Strong er er for me is the word er er for male because er (*for male?*) yes for male because er it er it a word, a very, er a very strong for, for, for (*laughter*) describe the, the meal, the male, er man (*mm*) and it's not right for a woman, it er right, er it er right er for a fem–, female, female er sweet or kind (*mm*) or love, er sweet, kind, careful (*yes*) er can, can describe very well of a, of a fem–, of a woman (*mm*).
W: But I think strong is er man, male.
M: Yes, strong (*yes*) is man (*yeah*), strong er hard-working (*yes*) because er is the man is er that work a lot (*laughter*) (*mm*).
W: But now, nowaday er female, female work more hard (*yes*) yes.
M: Hard-working, hard-working is for male because of the man (*yes*) work every time (*yes*) (*laughter*) not the woman (*but*). The man is er um, mine, er he works in my case he, he makes of er (*yes*) difficult, difficulter work (*yes*).
W: But housewife, housewife, housework is very hard (*yeah*), always cooking and cleaning and er washing (*laughter*) it's very hard.
M: Yes. And you said er that er hard-working is er for both yeah (*yes, both*). OK (*mm*). And other words such as loving (*loving*), intelligent, shy, logical (*mm*) are for both (*mm*) because in, er in, in the er man, in the woman er we, we can find love and intelligent (*mm*). The man er could, could er be shy or the woman could be shy (*laughter*) and er, or logical (*yes*) and yes but er other words such as sweet, careful and beautiful I think that, er (*female?*) that er are for the female (*um*), yes (*yes*). Mm, for you?
W: But some, sometimes er beautiful man (*beautiful man*) um yes, like a model (*laughter*).
M: I'm not sure I think beautiful er (*model*) is exact for describe a man (*laughter*), beautiful, but er yes, beautiful man (*laughter*) (*mm*) like me (*laughter*), like me (*mm*). I am, I am hard-

working, er I am beautiful (*laughter*), I am
strong. No. No, there are a lot of, of words
that can describes er every, every person, male
or er (*female?*) or female (*mm*), yes.

W: Mm. Yes.

Unit 15

2 Listening

1

Vanessa:

Well, I think my free time is for doing all the
things that I can't do when I'm at work like er
having fun, sleeping, relaxing, um doing
exercise or just generally winding down from
the day-to-day traumas of living. Er what do I
actually do in my free time? Well, I er play with
all my toys; I play with my guitar and the piano
and I play squash, and I read quite a lot and try
to improve my computer skills. That's about it
really.

Rod:

I guess I generally consider my free time to be
time where I can sort of indulge myself in
things that I, I like doing um away from work,
er, generally concerning er maybe myself but
also perhaps people who are around me er in a,
in a social, in a social sense. As to actually what I
do in that time, um I probably spend a lot of
time cooking and er that usually leads to social
gatherings, dinner parties or entertaining
generally and er I like to sit outside when the
weather's OK and have a few drinks and
chatting with people, so I guess I'm fairly much
a people person, so generally my free time isn't
always just to myself, there's usually others
around.

Derek:

So what do I think that my free time is for? Um
I think it's for doing all the things which you
always want to do but you can't do when
you're at work because you're not allowed to;
you can mix with the people which you want to
mix with um rather than those you're obliged
to, um and you can just basically be yourself
and relax and take things easy or you can try
and achieve things by having projects which
aren't related to what you do during the day,
um for example much of my free time at the
moment is taken up with trying to learn Danish;
um I'm also trying to master English grammar
and I also enjoy playing guitar, um going to the
gym and working out, things like that. Um

unfortunately I don't do as much with my free
time as I would like to do but I guess that's the
same for most people.

Sue:

What do I think my free time's for? I would like
it to mean time for me, time of course away
from work and away from all the duties that
one has to do outside work. I would like to be
able to have more time for me, more free time
to enjoy my family, but being a working wife I
actually find a lot of my free time is taken up by
doing the, er the domestic chores, doing the
gardening, and keeping the household running.
I do spend some time um on sports and leisure,
for example, swimming and playing tennis, um
and reading. I also find it quite important to be
outdoors so I do try and go for walks. Really it's
to do anything that's um outdoors.

6 Student language

1

Woman:

. . . and then swimming (*yeah*) and scuba diving
(*yeah, yeah*) and dancing, yeah.

Man:

Have you in Japan a very good, er places for
practise the skiing?

W: Yes, yes we have a lot (*yes a lot*). Yes, in
wintertime we can go, we can go everywhere
(*yeah*) er in the north of Japan (*mm*) yes, and
how about you? What, what is your favourite
hobby?

M: Yes, I like er so much to er play tennis (*tennis,
yeah*) um er skiing too (*skiing*) yes.

W: Can you ski in Spain?

M: Yes of course (*oh*). We have er a lot of
mountains in the north of Spain (*yes*) and we
can practise this sport er during the, er the
winter months (*mm*) and Easter month too (*oh
Easter month yes*) yes. Now you can, you can in
this, in this month, you can practise the skiing in
Spain in April (*oh*) yes (*even April*) yes (*I see*).
(*And then?*) and then er . . .

W: Um but my hobbies most of sports (*yeah*) so yes
I loved cooking (*yeah?*) yes, cooking (*cooking?*)
yes. I can —

M: I have, I haven't more and more hobbies
because I, I, I am a lazybones person (*laughter*)
yes, lazybones, yeah (*oh*); I don't like (*ah yes*) so
much the sports (*ah I see*). I prefer my house,
my friends (*yes, yes . . .*)

Answer key

Unit 1

1 Starter activities

2 Your answers here will depend on your interpretation of 'communicate'. You could tick everything if by 'communicate' you mean 'send messages'.

2 Reading

3 a) exchange trip   f) vocabulary
    b) performance   g) structures
    c) accent   h) average
    d) accuracy   i) improvement
    e) fluency   j) adjectives

4

Number of pupils tested	Just over 100
Number of groups in study	10
Age range of groups	13–14, 17–19
Amount of overall language improvement after stay of: • one month • less than one month	 20–25% 13.5%
Improvements in: • fluency • accuracy • vocabulary • accent	 15–19% 13.6–25% 17–49% 4.5%

4 Student language

1 They are talking about the hobbies they like and would like to do. They are intermediate level students.

5 Listening

1 Because it is about chimpanzees who communicate through a sign language.
2 a) chimpanzees b) Ameslan c) sign d) 55 e) grammar
    f) experiment g) unique h) English i) phonological

6 Speaking

2 *Agreement:* Right. Absolutely. Exactly. That's it.
    Disagreement: I doubt it. That's very unlikely. That's just not the case.
    I don't agree.

7 Classroom instructions

1 a) to b) you c) complete d) in e) could/would/can f) sure/certain
    g) for h) ask

8 Conclusions

  1 *Reading for detail:* 2.2, 2.4
     Work on word stress: 2.3
     Fluency practice: 1.2, 1.3, 2.1, 2.5, 3.1, 6.3
     Self-awareness activities: 4.4

     A gap-filling activity: 5.2, 7.1
     An opinion-gap activity: 6.3
     Letter writing: 3.2

Unit 2

2 Listening

  1 Emmah would probably agree with statements 1 and 6.

  2

The ways in which Emmah learnt French at school	The ways in which Emmah would like to learn French	
	At school	In France

Written work
Learning grammar
  by heart
Working from
  textbooks
	Pure French
	  conversations
	Writing essays
	Learning grammar
	  from essays
	Learning vocabulary
	  from phrase books
	  and dictionaries
		Live there
		  for a couple
		  of months

3 Speaking

  1 *Hesitation:* now, let me think
     Correcting yourself/rephrasing: I mean; sorry, what I meant to say was…; what I mean is; how can I put it?; or rather
     Stopping interruptions: hold on; just a minute; I just wanted to add

4 Student language

  1 It's about a good teacher.
  2 a) I had (a lot)
     b) very
     c) I've had
     d) self-confident
     e) went
     f) she was always trying/she always tried
     g) enjoyed
     h) the class to end
     i) something to someone
     j) to be taught/someone to teach it to me
  3 This student doesn't seem to have mastered the use of the following tenses: the present perfect, the past perfect, the past simple, the past continuous. This might be because:
     The student's own language may have different uses for the same forms of these tenses.
     The student's own language may have a different tense system.
     The student is unconsciously trying out all these tenses in order to master them and/or find out which are correctly used.

5 Grammar

  1 a) past b) finished c) use d) tense e) first f) actions g) past
     h) states i) going on/happening/taking place

7 Reading

    3 *spot* = improvised, unplanned, and on one point

      follow-up = leading on from/developing out of something done previously

    4 a) to get into a closed circle

        b) to hold a conversation

        c) to consult the teacher

        d) to play back a recording/a conversation

        e) to write up unfamiliar words/a conversation

        f) to play through a recording

        g) to do remedial teaching

8 Classroom instructions

    1 a) very/quite b) practice/activity c) get/split/divide d) give e) have/hold

        f) while/as g) want/need h) come

Unit 3

2 Reading

    1 He seems to quite like teaching and to enjoy a sense of achievement in his teaching. He would like another job, though less than before.

    2

Reasons for becoming a teacher	Short hours Long holidays Time to set up own business	Current teaching job	Primary- school teacher
Non-teaching jobs	Designer Set up handicraft workshop	Problems with teaching	Controlling pupils
Teacher training	Post-graduate teaching course	Pleasures from teaching	Better relationship with pupils
First teaching job	Small primary school in village	Future plans	Stay in same school

3 Grammar

    1 You could use *used to* in (b) but not *would* in (a). You could use the past simple tense in both (a) and (b), though it would not emphasise the shades of meaning that *used to* and *would* do.

    2 a) The rule for *used to* is false. *Used to* is used to refer to past habitual actions, states or situations that are no longer true in the present, i.e. it is used to emphasise the difference between past and present states or habitual actions.

        b) The rule for *would* is true.

4 Speaking

2 *Interest:* Really? Did you? Were you? Right.
Sympathy: I can imagine. How awful. That sounds dreadful. Oh dear. That must have been horrible.
Admiration: How amazing! That must have been really exciting. That sounds wonderful.

5 Student language

1 They're talking about past dates which are important to them. For Alberto it is his eighteenth birthday when his parents gave him a new car, and for Maki it is the date when she left Japan to come to the UK.

They were then asked to show their dates to one another. The person who *hadn't* written the date then had to try and remember what they were doing then and tell their partner. The partner who *had* written the date then went on to explain why the date was so important for them.

6 Listening

1

	Clare Boylan	Edna O'Brien	Dervla Murphy	Maeve Binchy
Their home environment	✓	✓		
Their first memory				✓
Their family	✓			
Their relationship with others	✓		✓	✓
Their pastimes	✓		✓	

2 *Clare Boylan, home environment:* urban Dublin; *family:* two older sisters; *relationship with others:* very close to sisters; *pastimes:* going to the movies, eating chips.
Edna O'Brien, home environment: a big house that was very beautiful.
Dervla Murphy, relationship with others: didn't make close childhood friends; *pastimes:* riding bike alone; reading outdoors.
Maeve Binchy, first memory: arrival of new sister – great disappointment – would have preferred a rabbit; *relationship with others:* her reaction to her mother's pregnancy and her sister's birth.

8 Classroom instructions

1 a) on b) passage c) pay d) about e) back f) through g) on
h) about i) to j) on

Unit 4

2 Listening

2

What their books contained	What their books didn't contain	What they learnt at school	What they didn't learn at school

Texts
Questions on
  texts
Grammar
  exercises
Vocabulary
  lists
	Communicative
	  activities
	Dialogues/
	  conversations
	Synonyms
	Definitions
	Opposites
	Gaps
	Collocations
		About the
		  system of
		  English
		How to
		  translate texts
		Information
		  about the
		  political
		  systems, the
		  history, and the
		  geography of
		  Great Britain
		  and the USA
			How to
			  understand
			  people
			How to talk
			  to English
			  people

3 a) coursebook
b) problem
c) grammar
d) exercise
e) communicative
f) activity
g) dialogue
h) conversation
i) interaction
j) synonym
k) definition
l) opposite
m) cassette
n) situation

3 Grammar

1 a) used
b) have taught
c) have never asked
d) didn't understand
e) asked
f) spoke
g) I have always believed
h) has become, wasn't

2 a) T b) F: The present perfect tense is used for states or actions that began in the past and continue in the present or continue to affect the present.

4 Reading

1 To help teachers choose a textbook.

3 The words in the questionnaire were:
syllabus   skills   attractive   coverage
balance   systematic layout

4

Verb	Noun	Positive adjective	Negative adjective
to suit	suitability	suitable	unsuitable
to attract	attraction attractiveness	attractive	unattractive
to accept	acceptance acceptability	acceptable	unacceptable
– – – – – –	appropriateness	appropriate	inappropriate
– – – – – –	relevance	relevant	irrelevant
to balance	balance	(well) balanced	unbalanced ill-balanced
to use	use	usable useful	unusable useless
to adapt	adaptation adaptability	adapted adaptable	unadapted unadaptable
to grade	grade	graded	ungraded
to structure	structure	(well) structured	unstructured

6 Speaking

2 Ways of changing the *subject*

8 Writing

1 a) to conclude: in conclusion, last of all, finally, lastly
   b) to sequence ideas: next, firstly, in conclusion, last of all, finally, lastly
   c) to make contrasts: on the one hand . . . on the other, however
   d) to refer to things: as far as X is concerned, with regard to X
   e) to join points together: both . . . and, not only . . . but also

9 Classroom instructions

1 a) you/us b) do/doing c) for d) stick/put e) so f) get/have g) OK/clear/all right h) afterwards/then i) on j) refer/go

Unit 5

2 Reading

1 *Possible answer:* It's about touching and its effects in the classroom.
2 The relationship between the teacher and the students.
3 a) watched b) asked c) just/only d) when/as e) concentration f) decreased

4 Because it reinforces the pleasure of being praised and praise then becomes more memorable.

5 *A lesson you enjoyed:* concentrate, praise, hard-working, Well done!
A lesson you found difficult: disruption, water-throwing, pencil-grabbing, bad behaviour

3 Grammar

1 The sentences in Group 1 use the present perfect tense to talk about an indefinite time in the past that leads up to the present.
The sentences in Group 2 talk about events in an unfinished past which leads up to and includes the present. The events also take place within a specified time frame.

2 The present perfect continuous tense is used for periods of limited duration that may have continued up to the recent present only. The present perfect is used for periods of longer duration that are probably still continuing.

4 Student language

1 The student seems to like devising and holding interviews, writing transcripts and listening to people.

5 Listening

1 They mention (a), (b), (c), (d), (f), and (i).

2 a) *introducing an idea/topic:* I think (line 2); I think the main thing is (lines 2–3); I often find that . . . (line 21); the other thing is (lines 37–8); I think it's also (line 49); another main thing (line 59)

   b) *drawing conclusions:* so (lines 37, 41, 63)

   c) *agreeing with someone:* yeah (line 9); sure (line 41); right (line 51); mm (line 63)

   d) *clarifying/expanding on something:* when I say 'fun' I mean that (line 10); maybe we could say that (line 14); I don't mean . . . but I think (lines 17–18); and also (line 37); I mean (line 58)

8 Classroom instructions

1 a) on   b) in/of   c) with   d) on   e) you   f) cross   g) got   h) ones

Unit 6

2 Listening

1 She mentions: pupils/children, colleagues, parents, classes, headmaster, school inspectors.

2 *Headmaster:* they hated one another
School inspector: once had an amusing experience when one visited her in her first job
Parents: thinks they must be involved in their children's education; tries to involve them
Classes: works very hard to achieve good class atmosphere
Pupils/children: need firmness to feel safe
Colleagues: objects to colleagues who put a strain on others

3 a) school inspector   d) children
   b) children   e) herself
   c) herself   f) colleagues

3 Grammar

1 a) who, that   b) who, that   c) that, whom, who, —   d) whom   e) who
f) who, that   g) who, that   h) that, who, whom, —
N.B. The use of relative pronouns is an area of the English language in which usage
is changing: *that*, as well as *who*, is used to refer to people, and there is a growing
tendency to use *who* rather than *whom* after prepositions.

2 i) c, h   ii) e   iii) a, b, c, f, g, h   iv) d

5 Reading

1 They are all about feelings and relationships.

2 *Text 1:* desperation, unhappiness
Text 2: guilt, desperation, anxiety, depression
Text 3: love, pride
Text 4: love, security, pride, admiration
Text 5: love, jealousy

6 Student language

2

Relationship	Female student	Male student
Parents	1	1
Boyfriend/girlfriend	2	5
Friends		
Neighbours	5	3
Other members of your family		2

8 Classroom instructions

1 a) I'd   b) on   c) make   d) for   e) against/next to/beside   f) on/about
g) us/everybody/everyone/the class/the others   h) piece/bit/sheet   i) by/on

9 Conclusions

1 *Possible answers:*
a) to stand up to someone/something   b) to be uninvolved in; to have nothing to
do with something   c) easygoing/lenient   d) to get on badly with someone
e) insecurity   f) shame/humility   g) to treat someone/something seriously; to
respect   h) calm; ease

Unit 7

2 Reading

1 *TD:* all of them; *TT:* 1: a language improvement course, 4: further
qualifications, 5: a methodology course.

3 a) TD   b) TT   c) TD   d) TD   e) TD   f) TT   g) TT   h) TT
i) TD   j) TT

4

Noun	Verb	Adjective(s)	Derived adjective(s)
development	develop	developed	undeveloped underdeveloped
training	train	trained	untrained
satisfaction	satisfy	satisfied	dissatisfied unsatisfied dissatisfactory unsatisfactory
education	educate	educated	uneducated
information	inform	(well) informed	uninformed ill-informed misinformed
support	support	(well) supported supportive	unsupported unsupportive
decision	decide	decided decisive	undecided indecisive
qualification	qualify	qualified	unqualified underqualified overqualified
dependence	depend	dependent	independent

3 Grammar

1 a) tell: Bubbles 2, 4   b) advise: 1, 3, 4   c) ask: 1, 5   d) suggest: 1, 3, 5, 6
e) encourage: 6   f) recommend: 3, 4   g) invite: 5   h) warn: 2

2 Sentences written for *tell, advise, ask, encourage, invite* and *warn* should be
followed by an object pronoun and the infinitive with *to*.
Those written for *suggest* and *recommend* can follow various patterns (see below).
Possible answers:

- I told her never to shout. / I advised her to always look relaxed. / I asked her to
  write an article with me. / I encouraged her to think positively. / I invited her to
  come and help me teach my classes. / I warned her never to lose her temper in
  class.
- I asked her if she needed a holiday. / I asked her to take a holiday.
- I suggested he should take a break. / I suggested to him that he should take a
  break. / I suggested to him to take a break. / I suggested his taking a break. /
  I suggested he took a break.
- I recommended he should apply for a course. / I recommended to him that he
  should apply for a course. / I recommended to him to apply for a course. / I
  recommended his taking a course. / I recommended he took a course.

3 ask, suggest, recommend

4 Student language

1 b, c, d, e

2 The writer's use of layout and paragraphing make the direction of the letter very clear. Although there are language mistakes, they are not sufficient to block communication.

3 a) for your kind offer to b) this c) have decided d) meet our needs
e) brush up f) could you come g) arrive at h) if this is inconvenient/isn't convenient

6 Speaking

2 a) 2 b) 3 c) 2 d) 1 e) 1 f) 1 g) 3 h) 2 i) 3 j) 3

3 *Suggestions:* Why don't we . . . ? What about . . . ? Shall we . . . ? How about . . . ? What if we . . . (instead)? Let's . . .
Preferences: I'd rather . . . ; I think . . . might be more . . . ; I'd quite like to . . . ; I'd much rather not; I'd prefer . . . ; I think I'd rather . . .

7 Listening

1 a) *to get into a rut:* to get stuck in a routine, to fall into a (very) repetitive pattern
b) *automatic:* performed unconsciously
c) *mechanical:* done without thinking
d) *formulaic:* following a set form
e) *ritual:* following an established pattern
f) *to lose touch with something:* to no longer have an understanding of
g) *to refresh:* to revive
h) *tacit knowledge:* what you know instinctively/without realising

2 b) *Possible answer:* They are central to the talk because they describe what can happen to one's teaching and how teacher development can help change this.

3 a) T b) T c) T d) F e) T f) T g) F h) T

9 Classroom instructions

1 a) for b) if/whether c) in d) Found/Got e) just f) anything g) play
h) false i) against/next to j) F k) ones

Unit 8

2 Reading

1 a) Better pupil–teacher relationships; incentives to do well; strict discipline; relevant punishment; more career information; school to be compulsory.

b) A new, modern school; free choice of subjects; good communication between pupils and teachers; fair rules.

c) School hours of 10 to 6; heated classrooms; decent P.E. equipment; understanding teachers; abolish R.E. and music; bring in life after school; no school uniforms; longer break times.

d) Enjoyable, useful subjects which are relevant to outside world; teachers who treat students respectfully and intelligently and who try to communicate with them.

2 Good relationships with teachers.

3 a) strict punishment/discipline
   b) to give a punishment/lines/
      incentives
   c) career information
   d) academic subject
   e) lenient punishment/discipline
   f) corporal punishment
   g) school uniform/subject/discipline
   h) decent P.E. equipment/relationship
   i) pupil–teacher relationship

3 Grammar

1 They are talking about something that might happen.

3 a) had   b) were   c) didn't teach   d) chose

4 *If* + the past tense + *would* + infinitive without *to*

4 Student language

a) He's generally quite satisfied with the school, though he's not too pleased with his accommodation or with the social activities the school provides.

b) *Possible answers:*

Dear Joan,

    Thank you for your letter ~~when~~ *which* I ~~recived~~ *received* from my teacher, I would ~~to~~ *like* to tell you my opinion about my school, The services ~~it is~~ *are* good, but the social activities ~~not to bad~~ *aren't so good* because the price for the trip~~s~~ ~~it's~~ *is* quit*e* high I hope *hoped they would be* to be cheap, ~~about~~ *As for* the accommodation it's good only the shower ~~it's~~ *is* bad because the water ~~it's~~ *is too* hot. there ~~isn't~~ *isn't any* cold water and *in* the kitchen there ~~no~~ *is* ~~kettle~~ *kettle* for a tea and suger and ~~mag~~ *a or mug* to drink tea, ~~That's~~ *That* is only *my only* my problem with the school.

      Thank you again   Faisal

7 Listening

3 and 4 For Emmah, the characteristics of a good teacher are:

being able to put yourself in the same position as/on the same level as the student / empathy with the student as someone who needs to have things explained
personality
a basic teaching knowledge
being able to help students rather than order them
kindness
patience
tolerance
pleasure in contact with others
sociability

5 Empathise with your students.

8 Classroom instructions

> **1** a) do   b) on   c) from   d) can/could   e) in   f) it/right   g) examples
> h) of   i) about

Unit 9

2 Listening

> **1** the importance of change in life
> **3** *Possible answers*: optimistic, dynamic, positive, determined
> **6** optimistic, simplistic, reckless, sympathetic, romantic, frustrated, realistic, determined, positive, hard-headed, dynamic, practical, idealistic, cynical, cautious, resigned, aggressive, pessimistic

3 Reading

> **1** *Possible answers:* resigned/sympathetic
> **2** Remembering their past lives.

4 Student language

> **1** optimistic/positive
>
> **2**

	Takako	Maria
Marriage	Wants to get married early	Yes – wants marriage
Children	Wants one or two	Wants four
Work/ Staying at home	Staying at home	Staying at home
Social life	Wants friend with children same age	

> **3** *Some reasons why Takako and Maria manage to communicate fully:*
> They seem to:
> a) listen attentively and with interest to one another.
> b) be willing to understand and try to make sense of one another.
> c) know one another and be good friends.
> d) make full use of the linguistic clues they are given.

5 Grammar

> **1** a) prediction   g) prediction
> b) prediction   h) plan/intention
> c) certainty   i) prediction
> d) plan/intention   j) prediction
> e) certainty   k) certainty
> f) plan/intention
>
> **2** a) *going to*
> b) *will* future (N.B. This is commonly used for predictions beginning with *I imagine, I suppose* or *I think*.)

c) present continuous tense. N.B. It is also possible to use the present simple tense to talk about personal certainties in the future. The meaning of this tense is slightly different to that of the present continuous however.
For example: *I'm giving up work next week* v *I give up work next week.*
The present continuous tense is used for future events that are the result of a present plan or programme. The present simple, however, is used for events that are predetermined by time/a timetable/the calendar or which are unalterable for some reason. i.e. with the present continuous tense the event is viewed as being under the speaker's control; with the present simple tense the event is viewed as being outside the speaker's control.

8 Classroom instructions

1 a) Right/OK   b) do   c) about   d) whether/if   e) divide/split/put   f) of
g) up   h) is

2 *A possible continuation:* 'Read it and make sure you understand it. If you have any questions, just ask me. (Pause) OK, now, read the information on the family. Right, so you've got two bits of reading to do; firstly, the background information and then the information about the family. OK? Right, I'll just give the sheets out.'

Unit 10

2 Reading

1 Anya is dissatisfied because of the poor pay, the lack of intellectual rewards, the difficulty of disciplining the children and the lack of resources. Olga is satisfied because she likes teaching and enjoys the freedom to teach how she wishes.

3 a) rowdy
b) teaching practice
c) non-rewarding
d) to keep at it
e) calibre
f) the basic rate of pay
g) to get by
h) unqualified
i) to carry on with something
j) to overcome
k) to be able to afford
l) to deserve

4 a) A + probably O
b) A
c) A
d) A + O
e) A + O
f) O
g) A + O
h) O
i) O
j) A

3 Grammar

1 Correct: c, d, e
Incorrect: a, b, f. These should read:
a) Job security is *as* important as good pay.
b) Long holidays are *more useful* than short working days.
f) *Rowdier* pupils tend to learn better.

2 a) T   b) T   c) F   d) T
Sentence (c) is false because other spelling changes can be required. If the short adjective contains a short vowel followed by a single final consonant, then that consonant doubles in its comparative or superlative form, e.g. *thin – thinner, fat – fatter, hot – hotter.*

5 Listening
    1 and 2 *Possible answers:*

Pupil–staff ratio	✓ 70 staff to 800 students Each class had/has two members of staff
Teacher development programmes	
Class size	✓ Set at 28, average 25
School resources	✓ Very good
Holidays	
Contact time	✓ Limited according to amount of marking required
Clerical support	✓ Decent support available
Mixed-ability classes	
Cover for absent colleagues	✓ Not obligatory, and paid
Paid maternity leave	
Form-filling	✓ None
Attendance in non-contact hours	✓ Not obligatory
Staff meetings	
School buildings	✓ Good quality
Paid lesson preparation time	

6 Student language
    1 The letter writer is interested in the jobs for EFL teachers.
    2 *Paragraph 1:* no   *Paragraph 2:* yes   *Paragraph 3:* yes
      Paragraph 1: the first sentence is inappropriate here.
    3 *Dear sir:* Dear Sir or Madam
      by the time: when/at the time
      that job of a teaching: the teaching job/post
      I've been teach: I've been teaching
      I would appreciate: I would appreciate it/I would be grateful
      if you sent me: if you could/would send me
      more details: further details
      in what concerns: concerning
      the payment: payment/the salary
      I thank you in anticipation: May I thank you in advance.
      Add in: *Yours faithfully.*

8 Classroom instructions
    a) which/what   b) stressed   c) given   d) mark   e) dot/mark   f) on
    g) check   h) as/when/while   i) that/everything

Unit 11

2 Reading

2

	Time
Teaching	9.15–10.30 a.m., 10.45 a.m.–12.00 p.m., 1.45–2.15 p.m., 2.30–3.00 p.m.
Preparation	7.30–8.30 a.m., 6.00–7.00 p.m.
Meetings	12.30–1.15 p.m., 3.30–5.30 p.m.
Other duties: Playground duty Swimming duties Seeing children go home	8.30–8.45 a.m. 1.15–1.45 p.m. 3.00–3.30 p.m.

3 Grammar

1 *Possible answers:*
   a) What time do you start/begin teaching?
   b) Did you do any preparation yesterday?
   c) Why do you have parent helpers?
   d) When do you do your preparation?
   e) Who made you think of teaching?
   f) Will you stay in teaching?

2 a) *Yes/No* questions: auxiliary + subject + infinitive without *to*
   b) *Wh*-questions: *wh*-word + auxiliary + subject + infinitive without *to*
   c) verbs *to be* and the modal verbs.
       To make questions with these verbs you invert the *subject* and the verb.

5 Student language

1 a) They're talking about stress.
   b) They are Swiss and Japanese.
   c) The Swiss speaker is probably a good intermediate student. It's hard to say what level the Japanese student is as she doesn't speak very much, though she certainly seems to understand what her partner says.

2 *Mistakes:*
   Normally you have moment for relaxing?
   Is not very busy in my country.
   From last October I haven't been in my country.
   Yes, is stress because I have to study another language.
   I was only beginner yet.
   I have to study a lot of.
   to work is very stress.
   You have to answer all telephone.
   You have talk with people, write a lot of noisy.
   For me work is a stress.
   I was secretary.
   I took a lot of stress.

now is a holiday for me.
write a computer.
I worked by insurance.
I had to read a lot of book.
I had to explain a customer about, for example, this insurance or that insurance.
was good, but maybe . . .
I get the chef, the company director, not very good.
I think he don't like me, and so, ooh, terrible!

7 Listening

1 a) ages   b) teaching   c) ways   d) activities   e) preparation
2 *Group 1:* b   *Group 2:* a   *Group 3:* c   *Group 4:* e   *Group 5:* d

3

1	4
reading	organising groups
number work	getting the apparatus ready
science	making paints and glue
art and craft	working in the evening
manipulative skills	and at weekends

2	5
mixed class	assembly
Reception and Year one	group activities
	story times
	P.E. times
	music times

3
project work
group work
whole-class work
individual work

8 Classroom instructions

1 a) some   b) in   c) out/you   d) columns   e) each   f) in   g) got   h) tell
i) boxes   j) By   k) can/could/would

Unit 12

2 Reading

1 *Possible answers:* her orderliness, regular attendance, appearance, clean smell, daily cuddles, interest in him, ability to listen
2 gentle, affectionate, dedicated, reliable, clean, ordered
3 gentleness   reliability
cheerfulness   cleanliness
affection   orderliness
sentimentality   liveliness
dedication
4 *Possible answers:* insecure, affectionate, sensitive

3 Grammar

1 a) she had not/hadn't been sweet-smelling.
  b) she had/she'd paid him less attention.
  c) she had not/hadn't loved teaching so much.
  d) she had/she'd behaved less reliably.
  e) she had not/hadn't looked like a giraffe.

3 c

4 Listening

2 behaviour, personality

3 *Behaviour:* nervous, eye contact, to fiddle with something, to grab a chair
  Qualifications: a diploma, a degree
  Personality: outgoing, ability to reflect

4

	Qualifications		
Behaviour	Inexperienced people	Experienced people	Personality
Not nervous all the time Makes eye contact	University degree Basic EFL qualification	University degree Advanced EFL qualification Possible master's degree in applied linguistics	Open Outgoing Enthusiastic Can talk intelligently about their experiences and hopes Able to reflect

6 Student language

1 a) The kinds of people they like and dislike.
  b) tenses, articles, word order, singulars and plurals, sentence formation

2 *Examples:*
  Tenses: now I study English; everybody don't come
  Pronunciation: sounds *r* for *l* (Engrand, crassroom); *d* for *r* (deserved)
  Articles: teacher is very kind; my classmate sometime go to restaurant
  Word order: I think here there is everybody is very friendly/ I dislike person
    . . . don't keep promise person
  Singulars and plurals: everyone help you
  Sentence formation: If you are someone don't keep promise; I think
    everybody here is very friendlier as every, everyone help you

8 Classroom instructions

1 a) to b) what c) through d) ones e) which/that/—
  f) against/next to/beside g) in h) So i) number

Unit 13

2 Reading

2 a) *Daniel:* objectionable, appealing, hurt, troublesome, unloved, angry, attention-seeking, caught in a vicious circle

b) *His brother:* better behaved

c) *His mother:* divorced

3 a) aggressive, objectionable, appealing

b) aggressive, jealous

c) jealousy of his brother, possibly his parents' divorce and/or his mother's behaviour

d) a mixture of giving him attention by talking to him or by reprimanding him

3 Grammar

1 a) — b) — c) the d) the e) The f) the g) the h) the i) — j) The k) the l) The m) the n) The o) the p) — q) the r) — s) the

2 a) specific b) already c) unique d) unspecified e) general

4 Speaking

2 *Possible answers:* To my mind . . . My view is . . . In my opinion . . . It seems to me that . . .

5 Listening

4 a), c), f), j), k), n)

5 The order suggested for these responses in the original article was as follows:

1 pausing

2 looking

3 pointing

4 naming

5 naming, pointing and looking

6 quiet private word (friendly or unfriendly)

7 restraining touch

8 specific prohibition (with or without sarcasm, smile, hostility or glee)

9 specific prohibition with unnamed (mysterious) sanction

10 public telling off/putting down

11 shouting

12 actual punishment, immediate or deferred, e.g. removal from room, detention, extra work, lines, letter home, sent to more senior staff

13 class punishment

6 Student language

1 • have a personal interest in students as human beings

• be well prepared

• be able to convey to students what he/she knows

• choose the most appropriate teaching methods

• be familiar with technological aids

• have good time management skills

8 Classroom instructions

1 a) have b) on/about c) checking/correcting/looking at d) in e) with f) case g) about/over h) on i) on/about j) everyone/body

Unit 14

2 Listening

1

Who are . . . ?	Girls	Boys
faster cleverer stronger nicer more talkative gentler better behaved	sometimes ✓ ✓ ✓ ✓	 sometimes ✓

2 He's five-and-three-quarters; he normally plays with boys; some of his friends are Thomas, Jamie, Guy, Sam and Harry.

3 a) He likes boys best. He's a boy.
   b) Boys can't have babies, girls can; there aren't many 'lady police'.
   c) They do the most powerful fighting.
   d) Because they're nicer and won't fight.

4 He can't pronounce /r/; he uses *why* for *because* ('Why God made it like that, didn't he?'); he makes a mistake with countables and uncountables ('not much lady polices'); he makes mistakes with a comparative ('dangerouser'); and a superlative ('powerfullest') adjective.

3 Grammar

1 Tag questions with a rising intonation. The most common grammatical pattern for tag questions is to put negative tags on positive statements, e.g. *It's raining, isn't it?* and positive tags on negative statements, e.g. *It isn't raining, is it?*

Another type of tag question is one in which the statement and the tag question are either both positive or both negative, e.g. *It's raining, is it?, So it isn't done, isn't it?* The function of this type of tag question is different from the more common one. The function of tag questions is normally to check/seek confirmation. This second type of tag question expresses a conclusion that the speaker has come to by judging the situation.

4 *Possible answers:*
She wanted to know | the names of his friends/what his friends' names were/are.
                    | the people he plays/played with.
                    | if/whether girls or boys were faster/cleverer, etc.

5 To make indirect questions you add a question verb (e.g. *to ask, want to know*, etc.) to a statement. This means that the question form in the original direct speech disappears, e.g. *'Where is he?' he asked* becomes *He asked where he is/was.*

In indirect questions you may also change the tense of the original question into a tense one step further into the past, e.g. the present tense into the past tense, or the past tense into the past perfect tense. Whether you change the tense or not depends on whether the state/event it refers to is still ongoing or not. If it is still ongoing you have the choice of changing or not changing the tense: e.g. *She asked Timothy what his name is/was.* If the state/event is no longer ongoing then the tense must change: e.g. *He asked her where she had been the day before.*

If the question in direct speech is a *yes/no* question, i.e. one introduced by an auxiliary rather than a *wh-* question, then you have to insert *if* or *whether* into the indirect question, e.g. *'Are you coming?' she asked* becomes *She asked if/whether I was coming.* N.B. *Whether* tends to be more formal than *if*.

5 Student language

1

	Italian male student	Japanese female student
Adjectives for males	strong hard-working	strong
Adjectives for females	sweet kind careful beautiful	
Adjectives for both	loving intelligent shy logical	hard-working beautiful

6 Reading

1 The original title for this article was 'Sexism in the schoolhouse'. This may not be the best title!

3 a) 1 Boys get all the attention.
2 Boys are asked to participate in everything.
3 Teachers call on boys much more often in elementary schools.
4 Teachers encourage boys more.
5 There is remedial teaching of reading for boys while there is no remedial maths teaching for girls.
6 Boys aren't penalised for calling out answers, whereas girls are.
7 The classroom presents a competitive model of learning which suits boys.
8 There is rising tolerance of male students' sexual harassment of female students.

b) Girls (1) show less confidence in their abilities, (2) have higher expectations of failure and (3) have more modest aspirations.

c) 1 Incorporating gender awareness into teacher training and classroom reviews.
2 Encouraging girls to participate more in maths and science.
3 Single-sex schools or sex segregation at crucial points in a girl's development.

8 Classroom instructions

1 a) with   b) blanks/gaps   c) corresponds   d) fill   e) explain   f) guess
g) have   h) for   i) pairs/groups   j) about   k) hand/give

Unit 15

1 Starter activities

1 1 watching television   2 computer games   3 knitting   4 fishing
5 playing chess   6 photography   7 playing the guitar   8 walking   9 reading
10 drinking/having coffee

2 Listening

1 See chart below.

2

	What free time is for	*What I actually do in my free time*
Vanessa	doing what you can't do at work, relaxing, having fun, sleeping, doing exercise, winding down	playing the guitar, playing the piano, playing squash, reading, improving computer skills
Rod	indulging yourself	cooking, entertaining, sitting outside drinking and chatting
Derek	doing what you can't do at work, mixing with people you want to mix with, being yourself, relaxing, having projects	studying Danish and English grammar, playing the guitar, working out at the gym
Sue	time for yourself, away from work and duties	domestic chores, gardening, swimming, tennis, reading, being outdoors, going for walks

4 Reading

2 *Possible answer:* . . . works hard at relaxing.

3 a) stressful   b) guilty   c) help   d) stress, health, relationships
e) addicted, effort   f) personal

4 *Stress:* to push yourself, intensive, to get to you, punishing, fast-paced, effort
Free time: relaxation, contemplative, time off, leisure, recreation

5 Grammar

1 a) need to   b) needn't   c) ought to, should   d) ought not to, shouldn't
e) may   f) must, have to   g) mustn't

6 *Student language*
    1 They both like skiing, but the woman also likes dancing, swimming, scuba diving and cooking, whereas the man likes tennis and being at home and with friends.
    2 The man mispronounces *favourite, Japan, skiing, mountains, months, lazybones, you.*
    The woman mispronounces *scuba, hobby, Spain.*

7 *Speaking*
    2 They are all used to link arguments.

8 *Classroom instructions*
    1 a) find/see   b) all   c) thing/step   d) through/all   e) that   f) another
    g) compare/see/discuss   h) change